Building the Web:
The Internet and the Property Profession

Dr Tim Dixon BA (Hons) DipDistEd FRICS
Director of Research

with an Introduction by
Richard Lay, President of the RICS

A College of Estate Management Research Report

September 1998   1998/2

Published September 1998
by The College of Estate Management
Whiteknights, Reading, Berkshire, RG6 6AW

ISBN 1 899769 52 8

INTRODUCTION BY THE RICS PRESIDENT

In my presidential address this year I stressed that in the very near future I believe surveyors are going to see their roles change in many key areas of practice. This is because, as we lose the monopoly of information we have held for so long, we will have to earn our living by becoming interpreters of information. The arrival of Internet technology is already making an impact on the way that retailers and the financial services sector conducts its business. The property professional's traditional role as 'information broker' will therefore come under increasing threat as we see more open access to property data and information for our existing clients, and also an increasing amount of research conducted by professionals via the Internet.

This research project holds valuable lessons for us all and is intended to help guide us over the next few years as professional practices of all sizes begin to appreciate the real benefits the Internet has to offer in sharpening the profession's competitive edge.

Richard N. Lay

July 1998

FOREWORD AND ACKNOWLEDGEMENTS

Until now, in the property profession, we have had to rely very much on anecdotal evidence to provide us with information on how far the Internet has penetrated into our professional work. The current research is intended to redress the balance, and is written with the aim of showing not only the potential benefits of the Internet and Intranets for organisations of all sizes, but also of providing an up-to-date snapshot of how it is impacting on the work of the property professional and on the property market itself. The research focuses on general practice and quantity surveying practices and corporates but the findings are relevant to the property profession as a whole and to a range of different sized property organisations.

My thanks are due to:

- All the respondents to the postal questionnaire and to the eight case study organisations and the participants in the interviews, who, for reasons of confidentiality, must remain anonymous.

- The following for their helpful comments:
    - Richard Honey and Faraz Baber, RICS;
    - Duncan Moir, Allsop and Co.; and,
    - Mike Brownlow, Jones Lang Wootton.

- My research staff who helped at various stages of the research:
    - Gaye Pottinger, Research Officer;
    - Jessica McGarty, Research Assistant; and,
    - Tim Richards, formerly Research Assistant (now at Jonathan Edwards)

- Alison Andrews, for her administration and help in typing the final report.

- The Print and Marketing Departments at The College for all their help.

- Rachel, my wife, for her help with the cover design.

- The RICS Education Trust and the Pat Allsop Charitable Trust for funding the research.

Dr Tim Dixon
Director of Research
College of Estate Management
Whiteknights
Reading RG6 6AW

Email: t.j.dixon@rdg.ac.uk

July 1998

EXECUTIVE SUMMARY

BUILDING THE WEB:
THE INTERNET AND THE PROPERTY PROFESSION

The rapid growth of the Internet and its increasing use in business and commerce has led many to argue it will also impact on the role of the property professional and influence future property markets. This research examined the current levels of Internet and Intranet access in a sample of general practice (GP) and quantity surveying (QS) practices and corporates, and investigated whether the Internet was affecting the traditional work of surveyors and clients' future property requirements. Although the profession compares favourably with general business and commerce in terms of Internet and Intranet access, smaller organisations continue to lag behind. By examining a range of different organisations, the nature of the 'drivers', 'barriers', and 'benefits' of Internet and Intranet use were identified. It is also clear that the surveyor's traditional role as information broker will come under threat in the mid to long term. The research (the results of which are applicable to other divisions and specialisms within the RICS) was conducted by Dr Tim Dixon in 1998 at The College of Estate Management, Reading.

- The levels of overall Internet and Intranet access of the sample compares favourably with previous surveys by the Department of Trade and Industry (1996-98) of general business access. The most rapid growth in Web sites and Intranets has occurred since 1995/96.

- The majority of respondents had access to the Internet but there were substantial differences in levels of access between organisations of different size and type. Smaller GP and QS practices, for example, had lower levels of access than larger practices, and corporates higher levels of access than GP and QS practices.

- Key drivers for Internet and Intranet use are support from senior management, an existing IT culture, a formal IT strategy and the involvement of all staff in the strategy or plan.

- Key barriers for Internet use are its perceived lack of speed and security, the legal and confidentiality issues surrounding information on the net, and the costs of access.

- The most important benefits of Internet access were increased competitive advantage, reduced direct communication and information sharing costs. Email's key advantage was its ability to increase efficiency.

- The conventional role of the surveyor as 'information broker' is not under immediate threat, and respondents did not believe the Internet would impact on location or the occupancy of clients in the short term. In the mid to long term, however, there would be an impact, and surveyors would also become 'interpreters' and 'managers' of more readily available information.

- Surveyors must understand and use the Internet to maintain their competitive edge. Marketing the business and the 'me too' syndrome were important factors influencing practices to set up Web sites, but there was considerable scepticism as to whether the Internet would be used directly and extensively for property deals.

Introduction and Background to the Study

In 1969 just four computers were connected world-wide to the Internet, but by 1984 this number had risen to 1000, and there are more than 10 million today. From its beginnings as an experiment funded by the US Department of Defence to develop computer networks that could withstand nuclear attack, the Internet has grown to be at the forefront of the 'Information Society' and a catalyst for the convergence of a number of technologies.

Today the Internet (comprising email and the World Wide Web) has expanded into the academic sector and ultimately the commercial and private sectors. Don Tapscott in his book 'Digital Economy' (1996) argues that new technology and business strategies are transforming not only business processes but also the way products and services are created and marketed, the structure and goals of the enterprise, the dynamics of competition, and the rules of business success. Two years later in 1998 the Clinton Administration and the USA Department of Commerce has heralded the emergence of the 'Digital Age' with a new report called 'The Emerging Digital Economy' and in the UK these developments have been mirrored by the Department of Trade and Industry's 'Information Society Initiative' (1996;1997;1998).

The reality of this is that although the digital revolution is beginning, growth is accelerating not only in the IT sector, but across all sectors of the economy as the numbers connected to the Internet also grow.

Many believe the Internet will have an impact on property and real estate (see for example Doherty (1996) and Lawson (1997). For example, email and the World Wide Web offer opportunities for the property profession to communicate more effectively, carry out research, and market the business as well as property itself. Certainly clients have increased expectations and demands as a result of using the Internet for themselves, and both general practice and quantity surveying Web sites have grown in number over the last 2-3 years.

Despite the wealth of survey data on the impact of the Internet on the business world in general, however, there is little or no research on how the Internet is impacting on the property profession.

The research project sought to answer the following questions:

- what is the level of Internet and Intranet usage and what are the attitudes of surveyors towards them?

- what are the 'critical success factors' (or 'drivers') which operate in enabling professional surveying practices of varying size to introduce and use the Internet in the best way?

- what are the 'barriers' to the successful introduction of the Internet and how can they be overcome?

- what are the key benefits for organisations using the Internet?

- how will the Internet affect professional work and the property requirements of clients?

The Technology Defined

The research examined both the Internet and Intranets.

The term 'Internet' is technically a contraction of 'international' and 'network' and is a world-wide network of computers. Key components of Internet technology include email (or electronic mail) and the World Wide Web (or 'Web'). The Web is the graphical front end of the Internet used for information retrieval and the RICS (1997b) has published a useful directory of Web sites for chartered surveyors.

Intranets are based on Web technology from the Internet, but applied to the internal network of organisations. They are centrally controlled and secure behind 'firewalls' (a computer server that separates the Intranet from the Internet) unlike the uncontrolled and anarchic Internet.

The Impact on Business and Commerce

Key features of the Internet are its ability to reduce the cost of marketing and customer information for businesses and the costs of distribution. In turn, this shapes the way the Internet is used by business and commerce to address a variety of consumer needs, which include:

- communications;

- publishing;

- distribution;

- marketing; and

- transactions (buying and selling).

Often, however, organisations do join the Internet without considering its role in their overall strategy.

McBride (1997) suggested a breakdown of usage to help organisations develop their Internet strategy. For example, opportunities offered by the Internet can be seen as a pyramid: at the bottom is its use as a basic source of information for ad hoc information retrieval and communication. As the Internet becomes more firmly fixed in the organisation it evolves into a business support structure for marketing, supplier and customer communications and transactions. At the highest level, the Internet may be used for revenue generation, and access and use of the Internet become a key part of the business strategy. Determining what level of dependency is appropriate for a business involves a detailed examination of the products and services and matching them to the Internet's structure and audience. Key questions to address in this respect include:

- is the company culturally suited to the Internet?

- is the information accessible on the Internet useful to the company?

- are the products suited to Internet access?

- is the Internet market suitable for the company?

Two surveys by the DTI (1997;1998) suggest the level of Internet use has grown rapidly in the UK and over the last 2-3 years. Some 49% of companies have Internet access in the UK, up from 35% in 1997.

The use of email is also highest within large companies, with 71% in the UK (DTI (1997)) using email, but only 16% of very small companies.

The same survey found that businesses are currently using the Internet for information access (91% of users in 1998) and email (75%). Other services and applications, such as purchasing, online sales and advertising/marketing are less extensively used.

The current use of Intranets is low in the UK - about 14% in 1998 (11% in 1997), of companies compared with 32% in Japan and 20% in the USA. Insufficient perceived benefits seems to be a major reason for this low uptake.

The Impact in the Property Profession

Levels of Internet and Intranet Access

Despite the recent RICS Survey (Honey (1997)), previous research had shown the property profession still coming to terms with IT. The current survey, however, confirms the view that as far as IT is concerned, most organisations (some 97% of the sample), whatever their size, now have access to IT.

Email access is commonplace in the property profession. Some 69% of respondents had access to email, and the primary use is 'communication with customers/clients' (81.7% of all cases). Access to the Web is provided in the majority (56.3%) of organisations, with 'research' (74.3% of cases) as the most important use overall. Some 34% of all organisations in the survey had a home page, and the figure was highest amongst corporates: 46.2%, compared with 33.6% GP and 26.6% QS. The period since 1995 had seen the most rapid growth in Web sites.

Only 16.9% of organisations had Intranets, and with Intranets the primary uses are 'company information' (80.9% of cases), and 'email' (66% of cases). The pattern of Intranet growth mirrors that of the Internet in the respondent sample with major growth occurring since 1995. Some 44% of corporates had Intranets.

Evolution and Use of the Internet

Two key reasons for developing a home page were marketing the organisation and the 'me too' syndrome, but it was important for practices to realise that, in particular, new clients would not be attracted exclusively from the Web. The personal nature of property was still vital to consider.

As far as marketing property on the Internet was concerned, this was more likely to succeed in residential than commercial, but even so was only part of the process of concluding a deal. Moreover, there was considerable scepticism over whether the Internet would ever be used extensively for deals. This was borne out by the fact that the Web was used predominantly for 'research' in 74.3% of cases, with property 'marketing/comparables' in 25.1% of cases (the lowest use overall).

The Impact on Professional Work

Email had made a substantial impact in all organisations. The most important reason for introducing email was 'to increase efficiency', and the case studies revealed that in the case of one QS firm nearly all drawings were sent on email and dedicated systems.

The postal survey revealed that surveyors:

- **do not** feel their role as 'information broker' is under threat;

- **do not** think the Internet will impact on the location and occupancy of businesses in the short term.

Surveyors **do** feel, however, that they should understand and use the Internet to maintain their competitive advantage.

Respondents did not feel that the information brokerage role of the GP and QS surveyor would be threatened in the short-term, but over the next 5-10 years the role of the surveyor would, inevitably, shift towards an 'interpreter' and 'manager' of information. In particular, 'disintermediation' could result in the residential agency market where Internet sales could increase. This should be tempered by the comments made about marketing property on the Internet, however. Moreover, property market imperfections would continue to prevent a serious erosion of the surveyor's role.

'Critical Success Factors' or 'Drivers'

The four most important drivers which promote Internet and Intranet use are:

'senior management support'

- 'existing IT culture';

- 'involvement of all staff'; and

- 'formal IT strategy.

It clearly is important to have support from the practice partnership or the board of directors in a company. The positive culture of IT in an organisation can also promote use. If organisations view IT as an important and vital tool they are more likely to use the Internet. Involving all staff in the implementation of the Internet means employees 'buy in' more readily to the new technology. Finally, a formal IT strategy, to which the Internet is linked, is important to have in place.

However, the size and type of organisation also plays a part: statistical testing revealed that larger organisations rated 'existing IT culture' and 'formal IT strategy' more highly than smaller ones, and that corporates felt the presence of a 'formal IT strategy' was more important than GP and QS.

Finally, security and Internet access were issues which it was important to deal with in implementing the Internet.

Barriers to Internet Use

The four most important barriers to Internet use were:

- 'speed';
- 'lack of security';
- 'legal/confidentiality issues'; and
- 'costs'.

However, 'time-consuming' and 'time-wasting' were also important.

These issues have often been raised in previous surveys (DTI (op. cit.)). The slow speed of Internet access poses particular problems where there is no dedicated link. Security issues, particularly in relation to the transmission of clients' details, were highlighted as a particular fear, and allied with this is the potential nefarious use by employees. Firewalls and Internet access policies can overcome such problems, however.

Again there were size and type of organisation differences: large organisations were more concerned about security than smaller ones, and corporates rated 'lack of security' and 'legal/confidentiality' issues more highly than QS and GP, which was a statistically significant result.

Benefits of Internet Use

The three most important benefits of Internet use were found to be:

- 'increased competitive advantage';
- 'reduced communication costs'; and
- 'reduced cost of sharing information'.

'Increased productivity' was also important. Maintaining a competitive edge had clearly been a major reason for developing company Web sites, as was shown by the case studies. Moreover email was a vital tool which reduced communication costs. Finally, email and the Web enable employees and clients to share information more easily than before.

None of the differences by size and type of organisation between various factors was found to be statistically significant.

The Importance of Size and Type of Organisation

Previous research has showed how Small and Medium Enterprises (SMEs) often failed to embrace the new technology. The results from the current research show that although small GP and QS practices do have access to IT they have still some way to go to embrace the Internet and Intranet to the same extent as larger practices.

For example, the current research found that statistically,

- the greater the size of organisation (of whatever type) the more likely it is to have email, Web and Intranet access, and

- corporates are more likely to have Intranet access that GP and QS.

For example, fewer smaller organisations had Web access than larger ones: eg 20.9% of small GP compared with 55.6% very large GP.

In many cases, corporates have the benefits of a well-developed IT culture so that the 'property department' of a large company has also 'bought into' the IT strategy and support. Professional practices often, however, lack these advantages, again because many of them are sole practitioners, and so factors such as the costs of Internet access can seem insurmountable to a company on a limited budget.

Conclusions and Implications

Comments from respondents' questionnaires and the case studies suggested there are two main initiatives that the RICS could develop:

- Further IT guidance and support for prospective Internet users. The RICS has a number of IT panels (for example, the Information Management Panel and Construction IT) and has developed an Information Markets Strategy (further information is at www.rics.org.uk). However, the property profession still lacks an overarching IT business support function. The Institute of Chartered Accountants in England and Wales, for example, has an IT Faculty (www.icaew.co.uk/depts/td/tditf/welcome.htm), which through its newsletter, booklets, bulletin boards and seminars, presents technical information for members at a low subscription; and,

- More information on how the Internet can help small practices, with perhaps a Web site providing relevant information and links to the DTI Information Society Initiative (ISI) and Internet information.

In addition, there should be a better way of accessing property information on the Web through a specialist search engine. Some sites such as the Property Information Mall and Focusnet go some way towards this but there is a lot of relevant property information that continues to be overlooked.

It is also very clear from this that small organisations, particularly in the GP and QS groups, have yet to be persuaded of the benefits of the Internet. Clearly some of the new technology such as Intranets will not benefit small organisations but email and Web access hold key benefits if a proper goal is set. The costs of getting onto the Internet are not high, but if a logical approach is adopted the rewards are there, and certainly more and more clients expect at least email access.

The DTI survey found that education and business support for small companies and SMEs was vital if the Internet and other technology was to penetrate successfully. It is clear from the current research that many larger organisations have used the Internet to maintain their competitive edge. Although the surveyor's role will not alter in the short term, a shift in emphasis will occur as Internet penetration increases, and, as a majority of respondents recognised, understanding and using the Internet is a key to the profession's development.

As one respondent, from a small practice, put it:

> 'Information is the key to make good business decisions and increasing market share. We plan to go onto the Internet in 1998 because we know we have to in order to remain competitive.'

About the Study

A literature review was undertaken to bring together previous theoretical and empirical work on the Internet and its impact in business and property. This helped refine the research questions and the main study was based on:

- a postal questionnaire of 671 GP and QS practices and corporates (i.e. corporate property owners, property companies, and financial institutions) and

- eight case study interviews with selected respondent organisations.

This was supported by a telephone survey to determine the level of non-response bias and by limited statistical testing. A response rate of 39% overall was achieved and the survey work carried out in March to May 1998.

CONTENTS

INTRODUCTION BY THE RICS PRESIDENT _____ I

FOREWORD AND ACKNOWLEDGEMENTS_____ III

EXECUTIVE SUMMARY _____ V

CONTENTS_____ XIII

LIST OF ABBREVIATIONS_____ XVIII

1. INTRODUCTION _____ 1

1.1 Background to the Current Research 1

1.2 Aims and Objectives.. 2

1.3 Methodology 2

1.4 Format of the Report 3

2. THE INTERNET AND ITS IMPACT IN BUSINESS AND
PROPERTY_____ 4

2.1 Introduction.. 4

2.2 The Information Society 4

2.3 The Internet: History and Development 7

2.4 How do the Internet and Intranets Work? 11

2.4.1 World Wide Web 11

2.4.2 Email 14

2.4.3 Intranets 15

2.5 How is the Internet being used in business?......................... 16

2.5.1 The Impact on Business and Commerce.......................... 16

2.5.2 Drivers and Barriers to Growth 19

2.5.3 Implementing the Internet.. 23

2.6 Surveys of Internet and Intranet Use................................... 24

2.6.1 Current Use 25

2.6.2 Size of Organisation 25

2.6.3 On-line Services: Current Applications 26

2.6.4 Future Developments 28

2.7 What is the Impact of the Internet on property?... 28

    2.7.1 Levels of IT and Internet Use 28

    2.7.2 Using the Internet in the Property Profession 29

    2.7.3 What are the implications of the Internet for the property
    profession?... 33

2.8 Summary and Conclusions.. 37

3. METHODOLOGY _____ 39

3.1 Introduction... 39

3.2 Identification of the Survey Sample 39

3.3 Research Design 41

    3.3.1 Postal Questionnaire 41

    3.3.2 Case Study Interviews.. 41

    3.3.3 Statistical Testing 42

4. RESULTS: QUESTIONNAIRE AND CASE STUDIES _____ 43

4.1 Introduction... 43

4.2 Questionnaire Sample, Size of Organisation and
Response Rates... 43

4.3 Questionnaire Results... 45

    4.3.1 PCs and Networking... 45

    4.3.2 The Internet.. 46

    4.3.3 World Wide Web (WWW) 48

    4.3.4 Intranets 50

    4.3.5 Barriers, Benefits and Drivers of the Internet/Intranet...................... 51

    4.3.6 The Impact of the Internet on the Surveying Profession.................... 54

    4.3.7 Other Issues 55

    4.3.8 Statistical Testing 55

4.4 Case Studies.. 57

    4.4.1 Evolution of the Internet 57

    4.4.2 Home Page 57

    4.4.3 Using the Internet and the Impact on Professional Work 59

    4.4.4 Critical Success Factors 61

    4.4.5 Future Developments 62

5. SUMMARY AND CONCLUSIONS_____ 64

5.1 Introduction... 64

5.2 Summary 64

5.2.1 IT Profile of the Property Profession.. 64

5.2.2 The Internet... 64

5.2.3 Intranets 65

5.2.4 Evolution and Use of the Internet... 65

5.2.5 The Impact on Professional Work 66

5.2.6 'Critical Success Factors' or 'Drivers'... 66

5.2.7 Barriers to Internet Use.. 67

5.2.8 Benefits of Internet Use.. 68

5.2.9 The Importance of Size and Type of Organisation 68

5.3 Conclusions and Implications **69**

5.3.1 Previous Research and Scope of Current Research......................... 69

5.3.2 Policy Implications 70

5.3.3 A Model of Drivers and Barriers.. 70

6. BIBLIOGRAPHY _____ **72**

APPENDICES _____ **75**

APPENDIX 1: QUESTIONNAIRE _____ **77**

APPENDIX 2: TABLES OF RESULTS _____ **83**

**APPENDIX 3: ADDITIONAL COMMENTS: POSTAL
QUESTIONNAIRE RESPONDENTS**_____ **107**

APPENDIX 4: CASE STUDY INTERVIEWS _____ **111**

FIGURES AND TABLES

Figure 2-1 The Converging Information Society (source: adapted from DTI (1997)). 5

Figure 2-2 Paths to the Information Society (source: adapted from DTI (1997))....... 5

Figure 2-3 Phases of Internet Evoution (source:adapted from Weintraut (1997))..... 8

Figure 2-4 The Internet Topography (adapted from DTI (1997))............................ 11

Figure 2-5 College of Estate Management Home Page.. 11

Figure 2-6 The Intranet (source:adapted from DTI (1997)) 15

Figure 2-7 Levels of Internet Dependency (after McBride (1997)) 18

Figure 2-8 Business Transformation through the New Media (after Tapscott (1996))18

Figure 2-9 Drivers of Demand for the Information Society (source: DTI (1997)) 19

Figure 2-10 Benefits of a Web-based environment (source: adapted from
www.cio.com) 21

Figure 2-11 Example of Home Page: Jones Lang Wootton 31

Figure 2-12 Example of Home Page: Property Information Mall 32

Figure 3-1 Size Distribution for GP and QS Firms: 1998 (source:RICS) 40

Figure 4-1 Sample by Organisation Type 44

Figure 4-2 Type of PC by Organisation Type 45

Figure 4-3 Presence of PCs 45

Figure 4-4 Reasons for Not Networking 46

Figure 4-5 Use of Email 47

Figure 4-6 Reasons for Email use 47

Figure 4-7 Reasons for Introducing Email 47

Figure 4-8 Access to World Wide Web 48

Figure 4-9 Use of World Wide Web 48

Figure 4-10 Presence of Web Site by Organisation Type 49

Figure 4-11 Growth of Web Sites by Organisation Type 50

Figure 4-12 Presence of Intranets by Organisation Type 50

Figure 4-13 Use of Intranets 51

Figure 4-14 Growth of Intranets 51

Figure 4-15 Barriers to Internet 52

Figure 4-16 Barriers to Internet Use 53

Figure 4-17 Benefits of Internet 53

Figure 4-18 Drivers for Internet/Intranets 54

Figure 4-19 Attitudes to the Impact of the Internet 54

Figure 5-1 Size Comparison of GP and QS Groups 69

Figure 5-2 Organisation Type Comparisons 69

Figure 5-3 A Simple Model of Drivers and Barriers 71

Table 2-1 Internet Applications and Uses (source: adapted from Cameron (1995)) 9

Table 2-2 Types of World Wide Web Servers (source: Cameron (1996)) 13

Table 2-3 Cost of Email Compared with Other Media (source: Cameron (1995)) ... 14

Table 2-4 Framework for Examining the Internet (source: Widdifield and Grover
(1995)) 17

Table 2-5 The Current Use of Internet Technology in GP Surveying (source: Honey
(1997)) 30

Table 3-1 RICS Member Organisations by Size and Type (source:RICS) 40

Table 3-2 Sample Details - Number of Organisations by Size and Type 40

Table 4-1 Response Rate by Type and Size of Organisation 43

Table 4-2 'Other' Barriers 52

Table 4-3 Chi-Square Results for Hypotheses 1 and 2 56

Table 4-4 Kruskal-Wallis Results for Hypotheses 3 and 5 56

Table 5-1 Comparison of DTI (1998) and Current Research 70

LIST OF ABBREVIATIONS

CSFs	Critical Success Factors
DTI	Department of Trade and Industry
EGi	Estates Gazette Interactive
FTP	File Transfer Protocol
HTTP	Hypertext Transfer Protocol
ICT	Information and Communications Technology
IRC	Internet Relay Chat
ISDN	Integrated Services Digital Network
ISP	Internet Service Provider
IT	Information Technology
PLT	Power Line Technology
SMEs	Small and Medium Enterprises
TCP/IP	Transmission Control Protocol/Internet Protocol
URL	Uniform Resource Locator
WWW	World Wide Web

1. INTRODUCTION

1.1 Background to the Current Research

In 1969 just four computers were connected to the Internet, but by 1984 this number had risen to 1000 and today the figure is more than 10 million. From its beginnings as an experiment funded by the US Department of Defence to develop computer networks that could withstand nuclear attack the Internet has grown to be at the forefront of the 'Information Society' and a catalyst for the convergence of a number of technologies.

Today the Internet (comprising email and the World Wide Web) has expanded into the academic sector and ultimately the commercial and private sectors. Don Tapscott in his book 'Digital Economy' (1996) argues that new technology and business strategies are transforming not only business processes but also the way products and services are created and marketed, the structure and goals of the enterprise, the dynamics of competition, and the rules of business success. Two years later, in 1998, the Clinton Administration and the USA Department of Commerce has heralded the emergence of the 'Digital Age' with a new report called 'The Emerging Digital Economy'. In the UK these developments have been mirrored by the Department of Trade and Industry's (DTI's) 'Information Society Initiative'.

The reality of this is that although the digital revolution is beginning, growth is accelerating not only in the IT sector, but across all sectors of the economy as the numbers connected to the Internet also grows. For example, the US Department of Commerce believes such growth will be driven by four types of economic activity:

- building over the Internet: some believe 1 billion will be connected to the Internet by 2005;

- electronic commerce amongst businesses: by 2002 the Internet may be used for more than $1 billion worth of commerce between businesses;

- the digital delivery of goods and services (eg software, newspapers and CDs); and

- the retail sale of tangible goods (eg PCs, cars, books, flowers and real estate).

Many believe the Internet will have an impact on property and real estate. For example, email and the World Wide Web offer opportunities for the property profession to communicate more effectively, carry out research, and market the business as well as property. Certainly clients have increased expectations and demands as a result of using the Internet for themselves, and both general practice and quantity surveying Web sites have grown in number over the last 2-3 years.

There is a school of thought that believes the Internet will impact not only on the work practices and organisational structures of property and surveying organisations, but also on the property market, and on occupier/client requirements. For example, 'disintermediation' may result as the surveyors' 'brokerage' and 'agency' roles become undermined by the greater availability of information on the Internet. The declining influence of distance on businesses (encapsulated by Frances Cairncross (1997) as 'The Death of Distance') brought about by the Internet, may also impact on the property requirements of major businesses and retailers. For example, the presence of High Street retailers on the Internet selling goods world-wide may lessen the need for locations in prime urban areas still further: in short, the move online may reduce the space needed for conventional shopping.

Despite the wealth of survey data on the impact of the Internet on the business world in general, however, there is little or no research on how the Internet is impacting on the property profession. The current research seeks to address this question.

1.2 Aims and Objectives

The overall aim of the current research is to provide a detailed study which reviews the impact of the Internet and Intranets on the property profession. In addition the key objectives of the research were to provide:

- an up-to-date survey on the usage and attitudes of surveyors towards the Internet and related technology, including Intranets;

- a clearer view of the 'critical success factors' (or 'drivers') which operate in enabling professional surveying practices or varying size to introduce and use the Internet in the most efficient and effective ways;

- a better understanding of the 'barriers' to the successful introduction of the Internet and how they may be overcome;

- a clearer understanding of the key benefits for organisations using the Internet; and,

- a better understanding of the Internet and its current and future impact on professional work, operational practice and property/client requirements.

In addition, some limited statistical testing was carried out to determine to what extent the size and type of organisation (and existing Web access) is associated with:

- email access;
- Web access;
- Intranet access;
- 'barriers' to Internet use;
- 'benefits' of Internet use; and
- 'drivers' for Internet use.

1.3 Methodology

The research was based on two main components:

- a postal questionnaire of 671 general practice and quantity surveying practices and corporates (ie. property owners, property companies, financial institutions and developers). This was carried out in March 1998 and the sample selected from the RICS database. An overall response rate of 39% was achieved. The postal questionnaire is included in Appendix 1 of this report.

- eight case study interviews carried out with selected organisations. The details are shown in Appendix 4.

1.4 Format of the Report

The report comprises:

Chapter 2:   which examines Internet and Intranet technology as part of the 'Information Society', and the development of email and the World Wide Web. The impact on business and commerce is also examined, together with the drivers and barriers to Internet growth. Previous theoretical and empirical survey work is also reviewed. Finally, the impact of the Internet on the property profession is investigated, and key research questions summarised as the backdrop to the research work.

Chapter 3:   which reviews the methodology adopted for the current research.

Chapter 4:   which sets out the detailed results of the questionnaire and case studies.

Chapter 5:   which provides a summary of the results and provides overall conclusions and policy implications together with a model of the Internet 'drivers' and 'barriers' for the property profession.

All Appendices appear in the yellow pages at the end of the report.

2. THE INTERNET AND ITS IMPACT IN BUSINESS AND PROPERTY

2.1 Introduction

This chapter sets the scene for the research findings which follow by examining the Internet and related technologies. The growth and evolution of the Internet are traced and the World Wide Web, email and Intranets described and explained.

The chapter also addresses how the Internet is impacting in business and commerce before looking at the drivers and barriers to growth. The chapter draws on previous empirical research by the Department of Trade and Industry, and from the theoretical work of others.

It also examines how the Internet is impacting on the property profession, and the likely impact on future professional work and property and client requirements, again based on previous, related literature.

Finally, the key themes emerging from the chapter are summarised to define the research questions which the current research addresses.

2.2 The Information Society

All over the developed world, changes in technology are making it much easier to access information using electronics and telecommunications. This trend is known by different names in different parts of the globe: for example in the USA, 'Information Superhighway' and in Canada, 'Information Highway'. The European Commission, on the other hand, uses the term 'Information Society', to emphasise the fact that the applications and development of information infrastructures will have a significant social and economic impact.

For example, in the UK, the Department of Trade and Industry's 'Information Society Initiative' (DTI, 1996 and 1997) uses the term to mean a society where individuals (whether consumers or employees) use information extensively. This has been brought about by the convergence and integration of three main business sectors (figure 2-1):

- the IT sector
- the telecommunications sector, and
- the information and entertainment sector.

An Information Society is one with the ability to access large quantities of information and entertainment on demand, to interact with data and manipulate large quantities of it, as well as transacting remotely and communicating on the move. Indeed, research by the DTI and Spectrum (op. cit.) has shown that although still an aspiration, there is rapid development towards the Information Society, along a variety of 'paths', as shown in figure 2-2.

The relative importance of these paths is not clear yet, and some paths may prove to be technological cul-de-sacs, such as the CTZ mobile phone technology of the 1980s in the UK. Others, such as the Internet path, may prove to be dominant.

Figure 2-1 The Converging Information Society (source: adapted from DTI (1997))

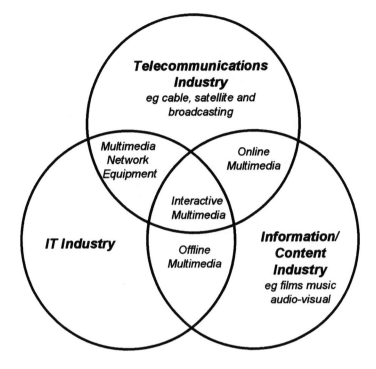

Figure 2-2 Paths to the Information Society (source: adapted from DTI (1997))

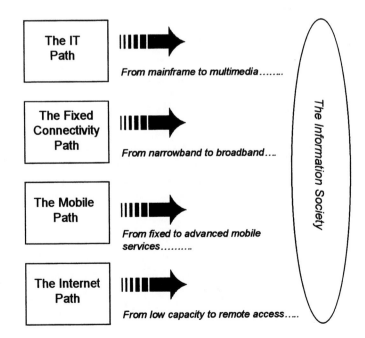

These developments have implications for business and society as a whole. The DTI (1997) believe these technologies can benefit a company's competitiveness in a number of ways, for example, by:

- improving business processes;

- changing business patterns and structures to increase efficiency; and

- creating new business opportunities.

This view is also supported by the NOP survey for the report, carried out in 1997, which shows that businesses accounting for 81% of employees in the UK recognise that the use of Information and Communications Technology (ICT) is important for competitiveness.

The Digital Age

Don Tapscott in his book 'Digital Economy' (1996) argues that new technology and business strategies are transforming not only business processes but also the way products and services are created and marketed, the structure and goals of the enterprise, the dynamics of competition, and the rules of business success.

What though are the features of Tapscott's seminal work? In fact he lists twelve overlapping themes that are emerging to differentiate the new economy from the old:

1. the new economy is a **knowledge** economy;

2. the new economy is a **digital** economy;

3. as information shifts from analog to digital physical things become **virtual**;

4. the new economy is **molecular** as organisations become disaggregated;

5. the new economy is a **networked** economy;

6. middlemen functions between producers and consumers are being eliminated through digital networks (**disintermediation**);

7. **convergence** between media is occurring;

8. the new economy is **innovation-based**;

9. in the new economy the **gap** between consumers and producers blurs;

10. **immediacy** is a key driver and variable in economic activity and business success;

11. the new economy is a **global** economy;

12. unprecedented **social issues** are beginning to arise, potentially causing massive trauma and conflict.

Expert commentators in the USA, such as Don Tapscott (1996), have suggested these developments are revolutionary, and in 1998 the Clinton Administration and the USA Department of Commerce heralded the emergence of the 'Digital Age' with a new report called 'The Emerging Digital Economy'. In the UK these developments have been mirrored by the Department of Trade and Industry's 'Information Society Initiative' (see section 2.6 of this report).

As Don Tapscott, a US presidential advisor on the information superhighway, suggests in his book 'The Digital Economy' (1996):xiii

'Today we are witnessing the early, turbulent days of a revolution as significant as any other in human history. A new medium of human communication is emerging, one which may prove to surpass all previous revolutions - in the printing press, telephone, television and computer - in its impact on our social and economic life. Interactive multimedia and the so-

called information highway, and its exemplar, the Internet, are enabling a new economy based on the networking of human intelligence.'

2.3 The Internet: History and Development

If the Internet is fundamental to the information society, what is it and why has it become so important?

In simple terms the Internet is a global network of interconnected computer systems which originated nearly 30 years ago, in 1969, when the US Government requested that computer engineers build a computer network which was fault-tolerant, decentralised and capable of surviving a nuclear attack. This network became known as ARPAnet and was soon connected to other networks, including universities.

Over the years since then the network has widened to allow further education and research traffic, as well as commercial use. This rapid growth was partly stimulated by the use of a standard industry communication protocol called TCP/IP (transmission control protocol/Internet protocol), which, after 1973 allowed computers and PCs anywhere in the world to communicate with each other seamlessly. Growth has also been promoted by the increased accessibility of PCs and modems to many more people, and the strong supply side expansion of businesses using the 'Net'. The Internet has a unique combination of features (Cairncross (1997)):

- it was largely a product of the public sector;
- it was ignored initially by the telephone industry;
- it is built on a single standard (TC/IP)
- the standard is public property;
- there is, as yet, no central control;
- American usage continues to dominate; and
- the World Wide Web is the driving force behind it (in 1995 it contributed one third of worldwide Internet traffic, by 1997 it was two thirds).

Today the Internet has some 100,000 networks worldwide, linking more than 40 million users who use the Internet in a number of ways including:

- communications;
- assessing databases and finding information;
- electronic transactions;
- marketing, and
- training/education.

Weintraut (1997) sees the Internet Revolution as forming three distinct phases since 1993 (or B.C., 'Before Communication'):

- Novelty
- Utility and Takeoff and
- Ubiquity, some time after the millennium.

This is shown in figure 2-3.

Figure 2-3 Phases of Internet Evoution (source:adapted from Weintraut (1997))

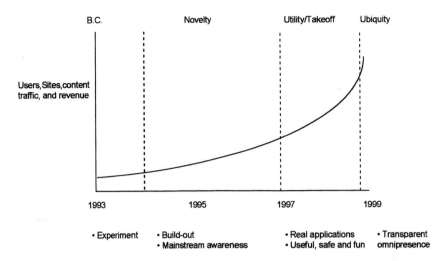

Table 2-1 shows the various Internet applications and corresponding uses. Of these the two most important are email and the World Wide Web.

Email has probably been the most useful and popular Internet service (Cairncross (1997)), and is almost as old as the Internet itself: the first electronic mail was sent in 1972. Today 200 million email messages are sent globally every day, and the DTI (1997) suggests that two-thirds of those using the Internet for email at work do not use any other feature.

Despite the growth of email it is only since 1993-94, with the development of the World Wide Web, that the Internet has acquired a large market, and it is only since then that most companies have begun to look at the Internet as a market-place. The Web (or World Wide Web) (WWW)) was invented in 1989 by Tim Berners Lee, a British researcher at CERN's European Laboratory for Particle Physics in Switzerland, and 4 years later, with the launch of Mosaic (a multimedia Web browser), use took off dramatically.

The Web has therefore allowed the Internet to work in new ways through the introduction of:

- multimedia, including colour pictures, music, moving images and data and text;

- hypertext which allows users to move between screens very easily by clicking a mouse on key words or pictures; and

- browsers (such as Netscape Navigator and Microsoft Explorer) which make it easy to use the Web.

In summary the Internet is a product of the same technological revolutions that have dramatically reduced the cost of delivering telephone calls and TV programmes and multiplied the capacity for both types of network. In contrast to the telephone and TV, however, it has no principal use: instead, it has many uses, including carrying telephone calls and TV programmes. As an open conduit, it can transmit anything that is digital, and this has also led a number of companies to develop private networks, or Intranets, for internal use using Internet-style protocols.

It is not possible to tell what the Internet will become because it is changing so fast, but it is an important technology. As Bill Gates (Chairman of

Microsoft) said, the Internet is 'the most important single development in the world of computing since the PC was introduced in 1981' (quoted in Cairncross (1997)). Its global reach, the way it is leading to a convergence of television and telephone, and its stimulus to innovation in the communications industry are all factors which show why it is important to understand how it is impacting on business and society as a whole.

Table 2-1 Internet Applications and Uses (source: adapted from Cameron (1995))

Application	Uses	Interface/Specialised Technology Needed
Electronic mail (Email)	Sending text and graphics to others on the worldwide Internet Encryption is optional Emerging uses: Electronic Data Interchange (EDI)	Internet email is generally text-based, although some email systems provide a 'what you see is what you get' (WYSIWYG) view of graphics, support attachments, and return receipts.
World Wide Web	Displaying hypertext multimedia information, including text, graphics, audio and video; users select hyperlinks to navigate; provides access to other Internet applications as well	Netscape and Microsoft Explorer are the primary graphic user interfaces, but other browsers are available.
	Emerging uses: electronic commerce, including order processing, can be used as a front-end to any application	Text-based browers (Lynx, for example) are also available.
Gopher	Browsing servers of menu-based information	Gopher client
Veronica	A tool for searching Gophers	Gopher client
Internet Relay Chat (IRC)	Online chat groups	IRC client
Usenet newsgroups and mailing lists	Discussion groups on literally thousands of topics	Newsreader
File Transfer Protocol (FTP)	Sending and retrieving text and binary files over the Internet	FTP client
Archie	A search facility for finding specific files and programs on the Internet which are then retrieved using FTP	Archie client optional

The History of the Internet

1969   ARPANET developed by the US Department of Defence which linked military and academic sites.

1973   The very first international links are developed to the UK and Norway from ARPANET.

1983   ARPA establishes TCP/IP (Transmission Control Protocol/Internet Protocol) as the standard for network information transmission.

1984   JANET (Joint Academic Network) established in UK.

1987   NSFNet created by US National Science Foundation to extend the network in the USA.

1992   World Wide Web established by CERN

1993   Mosaic, the first Web browser is launched.

1995   NSFNet wound down and commercial Internet takes off.

(Source: adapted from Bridges (1997) and KPMG (1997))

The Numbers Game - Facts about the Internet and the Web

'Measuring' Internet use is notoriously difficult because of its distributed nature. The lack of central control makes measurement difficult because some parts of the net choose to limit access by varying degrees. Instead 'estimation' is a more accurate term to use, particularly as surveys themselves often differ in the way in which Internet traffic is measured; for example, is traffic measured by 'page views' (the number of pages served by a site), or 'adviews' (the number of times ad banners are displayed)?

What is clear though is that both the Internet and Web are growing rapidly, and at an exponential rate. Commentators question how sustainable this growth is, and the 'Irresponsible Internet Statistics Generator' at www.anamorph.com offers a very sceptical view of future growth. The graph below, however, shows how rapidly and explosively the number of hosts (network computers that provide services for other computers) has grown over the period 1981-98.

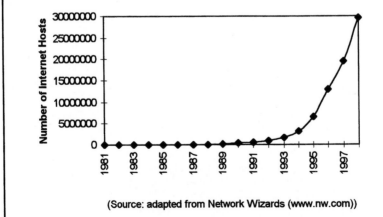

(Source: adapted from Network Wizards (www.nw.com))

2.4 How do the Internet and Intranets Work?

2.4.1 World Wide Web

The term 'Internet' (or 'Net') is technically a contraction of 'international' and 'network' (Kennedy (1998)). To connect a PC to the network requires a connection (usually through a modem) and a service provider (ISP). The 'topography' of the Internet is shown in figure 2-4.

As part of the Internet, the World Wide Web is based on hypertext links between various text and graphics images. This means that documents or 'pages' on the Web can be linked to each other by either coloured (highlighted) words or graphics, enabling the user to navigate or move from document to document within the network. This system also allows linkage to all information sources on the net, including Gopher menus, WAIS databases and FTP sites.

Figure 2-4 The Internet Topography (adapted from DTI (1997))

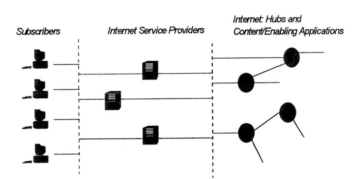

In other words, if a user logged onto The College of Estate Management home page (figure 2-5) by clicking the cursor on a keyword such as 'Newsletter', the next relevant page would be displayed. Users can then travel to a server somewhere else, indeed anywhere on the global network.

Figure 2-5 College of Estate Management Home Page

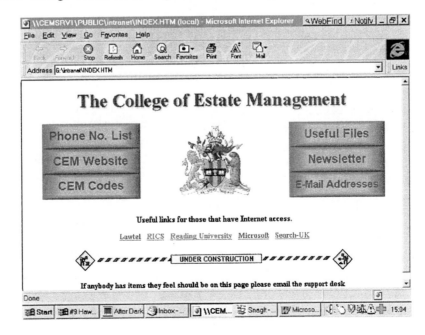

These actions are a way of retrieving information, so that users neither know nor care where the information resides, how it is stored, or what type of operating system the Web is using (Cameron (1995)). The Web handles this information seamlessly using a protocol called HyperText Transport Protocol (HTTP).

A key advantage to the user is that the Internet's packet-switching technology can compress more messages into the same space than a standard telephone call. Moreover, access is the cost of a local telephone call and the subscription fee to the Internet Service Provider (ISP). Furthermore, in the USA there is the added advantage of 'free' local calls (the price is included in the telephone subscription) and low ISP charges compared with many European countries.

The Web's ability to integrate many kinds of data, protocols and locations and its ease of use (through browsers) have led many businesses to develop home pages. For example, a chartered surveying practice would only have limited space in a marketing brochure to promote services, but a Web site can provide a substantial amount of information about the company, its services, and other related Web sites. Interactive Web pages can allow users to fill in forms that provide a single user interface for queries or mailing list databases. They can also have email addresses so that users who want to ask questions or send messages can do so.

The initial page of any Web site is called the home page and each page has a unique address, or Uniform Resource Locator (URL). For example, The College of Estate Management's home page has the following address:

http://www.cem.ac.uk

This can be broken down into two parts:

- **http://** which indicates the home page is a hypertext file located on the WWW; and

- **www.cem.ac.uk** which gives the **domain** as an academic (.ac) organisation in the UK (.uk) called 'cem' on the WWW.

The URL varies between organisation. A UK-based company would typically have an address such as **http://www.lloydsoflondon.co.uk**

In the USA, however, **.com** replaces **.co.uk** Increasingly, however, companies based outside the USA are adopting .com addresses to convey their international status.

It is not necessary to remember the address each time, however, because browsers have 'bookmarks' which can store favourite addresses for future use. Links or 'hot buttons' on home pages (these can be set to blue in Netscape), can be used to visit other home pages automatically. The CEM home page, for example, has links to the Department of Land Management and Development in the University of Reading, and to the RICS.

Supposing, however, that a user wants to find a particular address or find information on a certain subject. The WWW is growing so rapidly that this can be a major problem. Its speed of growth means that a published directory becomes out of date overnight. WWW technology has a neat solution to this by providing 'search engines' and 'virtual libraries'.

Search engines, such as Infoseek, Lycos, Webcrawler or Magellan can help enormously in the task of finding information; they comprise very large databases containing URLs and document samples. Virtual libraries, such as Yahoo and GNN, work in much the same way, but tend to preclassify the information by subject to make the search faster. Both search engines and virtual libraries are normally free of charge to use.

Growth in the Web has led to an enormous amount of available information. Table 2-2 shows the range of information available. However, a recent 1998 survey by Shelley Taylor and Associates (cited at www.nua.ie) of 100 of the world's biggest and most successful companies found evidence of poor navigation within sites. The survey took the responses of three types of user into account: customers, prospective employees and shareholders, but found that sites often catered for only one of the three groups. Site 'maps' appeared on only 38% of sites, for example.

Table 2-2 Types of World Wide Web Servers (source: Cameron (1996))

Most Common Types of World Wide Web Servers (January 1995)	
Topic	**Number of Servers**
Business	7060
Computers	2849
Education	1645
Entertainment	6863
Government	1099
Regional Information	3308
Science	2766
Most Popular Web Server Categories	
Topic	**Times Accessed through Yahoo**
Art	110,348
Entertainment	91,655
New HTML	46,435
Computers	41,930
Search	33,498
Society and Culture	32,822
Entertainment/Control-oriented Language	29,482
Computers/Multimedia	28,108
Entertainment/Dating	22,245
Business	19,143
Popular HTML	18,759

Despite such shortcomings, the Web has impacted on property and there is also a large amount of property and construction information on the Web. The RICS for example has produced a directory (RICS (1997a)) listing Web sites for chartered surveyors.

2.4.2 Email

'Email', or electronic mail, is probably the most frequently used tool on the Internet. Key advantages include its speed, convenience and cost. As Bowen (1997) suggests, it offers a number of advantages:

- it encourages brevity (usually!);
- it is easy to use;
- it is very fast;
- emails don't get lost; and,
- it is inexpensive.

In fact, email is the cheapest form of communication. Table 2-3 shows the relative cost of sending a two-page letter using various media.

Table 2-3 Cost of Email Compared with Other Media (source: Cameron (1995))

Method	Cost
Email	$0.33
Fax	$1.46
Telephone	$3.12
Courier	$8.5
Telex	$12.48

Email is a 'store and forward' media, because correspondence is possible with other people irrespective of the time zone or their physical presence. Cost is dependent on the Internet Service Provider, and, in general, Internet users pay for a connection to the network and not by the volume of messages sent.

Email also has disadvantages, however. For example, its coverage is still patchy outside North America and Europe; it is impersonal; and some dial-up connections may mean users are not prompted when email arrives or is sent.

Despite these problems, email is used not only for sending and receiving messages but also for retrieving files, documents and interrogating remote databases. Each email message consists of three parts: a header, a body and an end of message indicator, and individuals and organisations have email addresses to which these can be sent. A useful Web site for finding an email address is http://www.whowhere.com

Internet mail addresses are usually in the format, user@host, where 'user' is the sender's account name and 'host' is the computer server where the mail is collected.

2.4.3 Intranets

Intranets are based on technology from the Internet, but applied to the internal networks of organisations (Judge and Ogg (1997)). An Intranet enables a company to have a protected private network, but with selected access to the Internet and Internet style functions. It enables businesses to establish an environment like a corporate Web site, where its employees and others can access information and other services on the network (figure 2-6).

In essence, Intranets are organised, centrally controlled and secure behind corporate 'firewalls' (a computer server that separates the Intranet from the Internet), unlike the uncontrolled and 'anarchic' Internet (Szuprowicz (1997)). They need not necessarily be internal, however, and the term 'Extranet' has been used for Intranets which extend beyond the immediate company. For example, an Extranet includes direct links with other business partners or suppliers and customers.

Furthermore, the distinction between 'groupware' (or software designed to support group interaction) and Intranets (based on Web-based technology) has also started to blur with the emergence of Web-based groupware. Conventional groupware does not use Internet protocols and is proprietary, which makes linkage between other companies and partners more difficult. Groupware products, such as Lotus Notes, however, have been developed to link more effectively with Web technology.

Figure 2-6 The Intranet (source:adapted from DTI (1997))

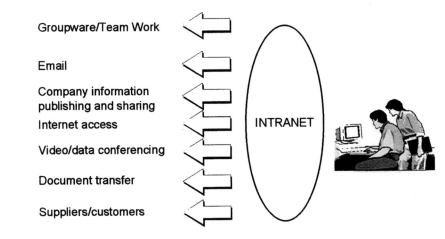

Factors such as flattened management structures, the increasing trend towards globalisation, the increased need to link with customers and suppliers and the exploitation of information as a key business resource have all contributed to the emergence of Intranets (Judge and Ogg (1997)). In addition, Intranets offer advantages over traditional network software (Bowen, op. cit.):

- multimedia is brought to every computer and the combination of Web browsers and high band width internal networks provides opportunities for video links and online meetings;

- they are easy to use;

- they are usually linked to the Internet, which means users can send email and use the Web;

- they are cheap because they are based on browser software;

- they work on independent hardware platforms.

A recent report (Durlacher (1997)) cited in DTI (1997) found that 13% of the UK's top 1000 companies have an Intranet, and 67% of US companies are deploying or planning to deploy an Intranet.

2.5 How is the Internet being used in business?

2.5.1 The Impact on Business and Commerce

Key features of the Internet are its ability to reduce the cost of marketing and customer information for businesses and the costs of distribution. In turn, this shapes the way the Internet is used by business and commerce to address a variety of consumer needs, which include:

- communications;

- publishing;

- distribution;

- marketing; and

- transactions (buying and selling).

Some commentators see the Internet as changing the very nature and structure of organisations. For example, Evans and Wurster (1997) argue that the Internet allows businesses to unbundle information from the physical value chain to create not only a new information business, but also a streamlined physical one. Where interactive personal selling is *de rigeur* (such as insurance, real estate and travel) then such changes could well occur over the next 5-10 years. This has already happened in banking in the USA where the Internet is giving customers direct access to service providers: the retail bank therefore no longer stands between the customer and the full range of financial services. Much more fluid channels are opened up by technologies such as the Web, which Evans and Wurster term a 'hyperarchy', where everyone communicates with everyone else on the basis of shared standards.

These changes in communication come at a time when other trends are occurring in the corporate world. An example is the impact of globalisation, with worldwide trade and investment affecting pan-national economic trends and activity. This has been coupled with the booming market for creative ideas and the ability to process information rapidly. Low inflation and cost reduction have become ingrained in companies' psyches and this in turn has led to businesses cutting back on middle management layers and external layers (intermediaries). 'Flatter' organisations are therefore increasingly commonplace. Indeed Francis Cairncross (op. cit.) sees this as just one facet of what she calls 'The Death of Distance': distance will no longer be a major limitation for businesses or individuals because of technology and competition in telecommunications.

Widdifield and Grover (1995) suggest a more detailed framework for identifying and evaluating the opportunities presented by the Internet. This is shown in Table 2-4. The impact on business is divided into three major areas:

- compression of time;

- overcoming geographical restrictions; and

- restructuring relationships.

Table 2-4 Framework for Examining the Internet (source: Widdifield and Grover (1995))

Business Impact and Business Value	Compression of Time	Overcoming Geographical Restrictions	Restructuring Relationships
Efficiency	Accelerate Processes	Economies of Scale	Bypass Intermediaries
Effectiveness	Reduce Float	Global Control	Replicate Scarce Knowledge
Innovation	Service Excellence	New Markets	Build Umbilical Cords

Given that business value can be represented by increased operating efficiency, improved business effectiveness or a basic transformation (innovation) of a firm's business functions, each impact/business value pair in the grid defines a particular Internet application together with a set of implementation issues.

For example, the Internet can widen the span of management control within a firm by allowing intermediaries to be bypassed - customer service can be improved by more direct contact with the person likely to fulfil their request, and this is known as 'disintermediation' (see section 2.7.3 below). The Internet can also make data, especially from remote sources, more rapidly available to decision makers by reducing information 'float' (i.e. the time taken to collect, manipulate and present raw data for decisions). The Internet can also build 'umbilical cords' with customers by bringing them closer to the company and its information sources.

Often, however, organisations do join the Internet without considering its role in their overall strategy. McBride (1997) suggested a breakdown of usage to help organisations develop their strategy. For example, opportunities offered by the Internet can be seen as a pyramid (figure 2-7): at the bottom is its use as a basic source of information for ad hoc information retrieval and communication. As the Internet becomes more firmly fixed in the organisation it evolves into a business support structure for marketing, supplier and customer communications and transactions. At the highest level, the Internet may be used for revenue generation, and access and use of the Internet become a key part of the business strategy. Determining what level of dependency is appropriate for a business involves a detailed examination of the products and services and matching them to the Internet's structure and audience. Key questions to address in this respect include:

- is the company culturally suited to the Internet?

- is the information accessible on the Internet useful to the company?

- are the products suited to Internet access?

- is the Internet market suitable for the company?

Figure 2-7 Levels of Internet Dependency (after McBride (1997))

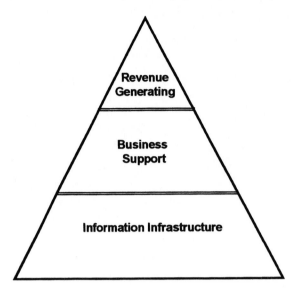

Tapscott (1996) takes a higher level view of the transformations brought about by new media including the Internet. He argues that the economy is moving from one based on the firm to one based on networks: the model for this operates at five levels (see figure 2-8), and at each level there is an enabling technology and a fundamental change in the nature of work occurring. Tapscott cites examples of 'Internetworked building groups' from the USA: for example, the customised design of houses between architect and client using virtual reality; the transmission of drawings and documents on the Web and the despatch of materials for final assembly on site in a matter of weeks. This is part of Tapscott's 'Digital Age' concept.

Figure 2-8 Business Transformation through the New Media (after Tapscott (1996))

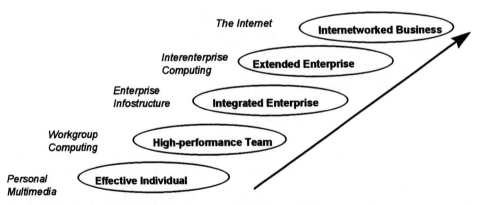

Developing an IT strategy, which should include systems, management and technology, is therefore vital in this respect (Earl (1989)). As Garvey (1997) points out, the failure rate of Internet sites is some 50%, and there has been a tendency for companies to rush into the new technology. He suggests there are three golden rules for a successful Intranet strategy, but the rules also hold true for the Internet as well:

- adopt a long term vision for corporate use, by starting with a business audit;

- create a culture of information ownership, and

- recognise, adapt to, and take advantage of the inherent qualities of electronic information.

These issues are examined in more detail in section 2.5.3 below.

2.5.2 *Drivers and Barriers to Growth*

At a macro level there are a number of factors that could stimulate a rapid move towards the Information Society, or lead to constraints: these apply to all information and communications technology, including the Internet (DTI (1997)) (figure 2-9).

Ultimately, the enhanced utility that ICT will deliver to business and customers is the most important driver. But other basic requirements are:

- sufficient income to purchase goods and services;

- access to advanced infrastructure able to support a wide range of services;

- access to electronic content; and,

- strong local supply of ICT services.

On the demand side, the 'culture' or attitude of society also impacts on the speed of development. The DTI (1996) defines this as the willingness to innovate, language, education, government structures and the longevity of the competitive marketplace.

Figure 2-9 Drivers of Demand for the Information Society (source: DTI (1997))

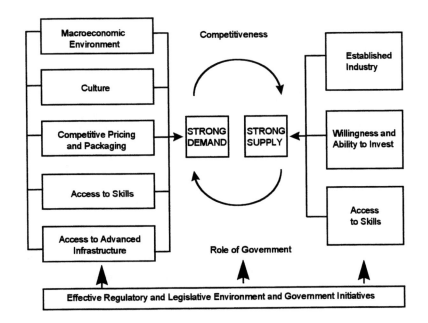

The 1997 and 1998 DTI surveys found that the following factors were barriers to growth:

- negative attitudes to ICT;

- a low skills base;

- high prices; and,

- absence of infrastructure.

The DTI (1997) research showed, for example, that a major constraint encountered by governments seeking to move towards the information society is a lack of understanding, which falls into two categories:

- a failure to grasp the concept of the Information Society and to appreciate the benefits offered by ICT;

- a failure to understand how to implement and use specific technologies. This is the result of ICT often being a specialist preserve in arguments with a lack of mass appeal, and companies, particularly smaller SMEs, not having ready access to experienced users.

Further evidence supports this view. For example, the Spectrum Business Survey in the DTI (1998) report found that in the UK, 43% of companies believed that their employees do not have sufficient IT skills to maximise the competitive advantages of ICTs. This had fallen from 52% in 1997, but in 1998 only 33% of companies in UK trained 'frequently' or 'quite often' in IT. This was reflected in uncertain attitudes towards ICT, particularly by SMEs. Often age, position in a company, education and past experience influence attitudes towards ICT. Older, senior managers may well have a negative attitude and the 1998 DTI survey cites a Bathwick (1998) report which suggested that only 64% of senior executives of large UK companies use a PC at work.

High prices were also cited as a barrier. Although ICT prices continue to fall, software prices and operational costs may prove excessive for small companies. The cost of network connections may have a substantial impact on SMEs, for example.

Infrastructure access is a particular issue for the Internet and the 1997 NOP survey (DTI (1998)) showed that more than 50% of UK Internet users were dissatisfied with the speed of downloading pages and graphics.

There have been a number of recent government initiatives in the UK to promote the Information Society and overcome the barriers. These include:

- *DTI's Information Society Initiative (ISI),* aimed at encouraging business to take full advantage of the range of new ways to access, use and send information. It brings together a range of programmes in support of UK companies, especially those who may be inexperienced in the use of new technologies.

- *IT for All,* which is a four year initiative launched in 1996 and designed to increase the level of awareness amongst UK adults of the benefits of IT;

- *Connecting the Learning Society* (DFEE (1997)), which is a consultation paper promoting the idea of a national grid for learning linking all schools, colleges, universities and libraries in the UK by 2002; and

- *The UK Enterprise Zone*, which was developed by the DTI in 1997, and is designed to guide SMEs to the most suitable Web sites (www.enterprisezone.org.uk).

These drivers and barriers to growth act at a macro level, but also act at an organisational level for particular technologies. Moreover, the Internet and Intranets offer a number of tangible and intangible benefits which themselves act as drivers. For example, tangible benefits include:

- the use of open standards which promote quick and effective dissemination of data;

- reduced costs of information extraction;

- better communications; and

- information sharing and collaborative working.

Intangible benefits might include:

- a changed corporate culture, and

- opportunities for business re-engineering.

The advantages of a Web-based environment are shown in Figure 2-10.

The 1997 and 1998 DTI surveys also found that company Internet access is in fact higher in countries with a high consumer penetration of the Internet, indicating that a wider familiarity with the technology in the country links with usage at work.

Figure 2-10 Benefits of a Web-based environment (source: adapted from www.cio.com)

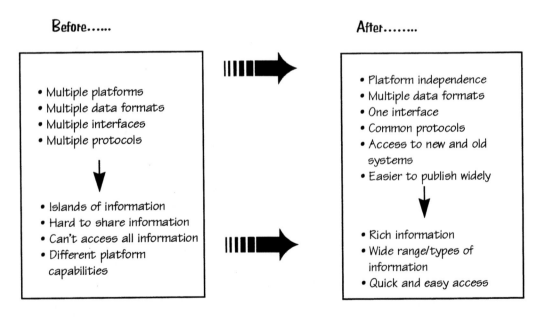

However, there are also constraints and barriers to growth for the Internet. These include:

- band width and speed of access (ie 'Web lag');

- security risks;

- content regulation, and

- pricing constraints.

For example, increased bandwidth (or the capacity of a telecommunications link) is a critical factor for Internet growth and perhaps the greatest constraint. Lack of bandwidth constrains the number of uses and the speed at which data can be transmitted.

Home shopping and home banking using the Internet have also led to concerns over security, particularly credit card fraud, although 'encryption' (or coding) has helped resolve a number of concerns. Related to this are fears over downloading viruses from the Internet, but again anti-virus software has alleviated such problems.

Worry over the content of some material on the Internet has also been voiced, particularly the free availability of pornography. The US Government has adopted a tough regime by mandating the use of special V-chips to control downloading, but in the UK a more self-regulatory approach exists.

Finally, the cost of hardware and connection charges may still be a barrier for some organisations, particularly SMEs and low income households.

Doherty (1997) indicates that there are three main areas of concern about the use of the Internet:

- are employees using the Internet productively or efficiently?

- could the Internet be used within the company to compromise its business interests?

- is Internet usage in a company illegal, and could it leave it open to liability?

Time wasting on the Internet by staff is a source of major concern for businesses, as a report by Aspect Consulting called 'Access Control Time Bomb' (1996) pointed out: the report found that 59% of decision makers in Europe found surfing for personal use totally unacceptable during core business time. Other surveys suggest that more managers are now concerned about time wasting on the Internet than about security, although some companies adopt a liberal attitude by encouraging surfing to promote Web skills. Bowen (op. cit.) suggests there are three access options:

- using technology to control access for different levels of employee;

- rely on training and trust;or

- combining the two.

Other issues also need to be considered. For example, for a design and construction business there are further liability issues which may need to be addressed when transferring project information to clients, including errors in the information sent and controlling the ownership of material and its reuse.

This is why it is important to develop an IT strategy in implementing the Internet which incorporates a company-wide policy on such issues as security of confidential client information, training, limiting access for employees and controlling content.

2.5.3 *Implementing the Internet*

There is a growing body of theory and empirical evidence which reinforces the view that an IT strategy and an organisation's corporate strategy should be closely linked. For example, research by Kearney (1984) found there was a strong link between business performance and IT success: moreover 40% of successful user companies developed their IT strategy from the business plan, and promoted the influence of the latter by the former. Although it is difficult to establish a definite cause and effect relationship, the evidence does point to a link.

As Doherty (1997) points out, applying any form of IT correctly involves 'planning' and planning is part of a strategy. Glueck (1980) for example defines strategy as a *'unified, comprehensive and integrated plan ... designed to ensure that the basic objectives of the enterprise are achieved.'* In terms of an IT strategy this will mean incorporating three main elements (Earl (1989)):

- systems (the application to be computerised);

- technology (or how the strategy is to be delivered); and

- management, with the policies (including training and education) procedures, aims and actions needed to implement the policy.

Frameworks such as Potter's (1980) model of competition have been developed to provide methods for analysing the strategic impact of IT. Others adopt a more prescriptive approach. Hargitay and Dixon (1989), for example, suggest a simple systematic approach to selecting any IT system:

- Stage 1   -   Feasibility analysis, including

  - business needs analysis;

  - the type of application; and,

  - detailed requirements.

- Stage 2   -   Investigation, including market evaluations and demonstrations.

- Stage 3   -   Implementation, which involves selection and choice of the new system.

Implementing the Internet also implies a strategic approach. At a basic level this means understanding the work process involved. Doherty (op. cit.) suggests piloting the Internet within the business first (as an Intranet) before connecting to the outside world. Benchmarking is a vital step to beginning implementation: comparison with others in the same industry and with those outside will be an important way of setting up a standard for measuring progress. In this sense, Doherty sees companies evolving in a three-stage process:

- Stage 1:   'computer-aided business', where manual tasks are automated;

- Stage 2:   'computer-integrated business', where sharing of information occurs;

- Stage 3: 'collaboration', with information sharing within and without the business.

KPMG (1996) suggest that providing access to the Internet includes the following stages:

- assessing requirements: who needs access and why?

- setting a security policy for incoming and outgoing traffic and which users are entitled to use which applications; and

- selecting an appropriate service provider and configuring the company network.

In terms of WWW provision, KPMG have also identified three distinct phases in companies:

- the 'R&D phase' where projects proceed on a short-term experimental basis often driven by the IT or marketing departments, which then provides a prototype and, finally, evolution into the service. In this first stage there are usually no defined processes and there is often a lack of long-term planning. Costs are in the range £5,000-20,000.

- In the 'prototype phase' the main driver is support from a senior executive in the firm. There is usually much agonising as to whether to develop the home page in-house or externally. Content and image become more sophisticated and the costs are higher: £30,000-200,000 for an in-house operation.

- The 'final phase' includes several key features:

  -a business strategy linked to the IT component;

  -redesigned process streams to support the electronic channels more efficiently;

  -reworked roles and responsibilities to support the new electric communications;

  -a quality system to support the time, compression and high expectation of customers or suppliers connected electronically to the company;

  -the reorientation of back-end systems to serve and be served by the new electronic links.

The final phase involves substantial transformation of the business and costs could range from £200,000 to £2 million plus.

2.6 Surveys of Internet and Intranet Use

There have been a very large number of surveys of both Internet and Intranet usage which have rapidly became dated as a result of the changing technology. However, a number of surveys are updated regularly and the results are available at a variety of Web sites. The following section distils the main findings from five major published surveys:

- *'Moving into the Information Society - An International Benchmarking Study'* (DTI (1997)). This was a major survey of five EU countries carried out in 1997 by NOP;

- *'Moving into the Information Age - International Benchmarking Study'* (DTI (1998)). This was the follow-up study to the 1997 survey;

- *NOP Business and Home User Internet Surveys 1997.* These are the latest of NOPs ongoing 'Waves' of Internet Survey Usage;

- *CyberKix's 1996 study: 'How UK SMEs are Implementing the Internet';* and

- *CMG's 1997 UK Intranet Survey.*

These surveys indicate a number of themes and recurring issues.

2.6.1 Current Use

Internet use within the USA has become standard for many businesses and the DTI survey showed that 57% of companies in the USA had Internet access in 1998 (51% in 1997). The figure is 49% for the UK (35% in 1997), 44% in Germany (27% in 1997), but only 24% in France (13% in 1997). Size differences are important (see section 2.6.2 below), but there has certainly been rapid growth from 1997-98. Japan now has the highest Internet access amongst companies - 73% compared with 63% in 1997.

The use of email is also highest within large companies, with 71% in the UK (DTI (1997)) using email, but only 16% of very small companies. Despite less widespread email use in comparison with the USA, the UK uses email quite intensively. Internal email communication within the same site and between sites remains the primary area of usage (68% and 68% respectively in the UK in 1998). Communications with customers and suppliers is also becoming important, however (62% and 54% respectively in the UK in 1998).

The same survey found that businesses are currently using the Internet for information access (91% of users in 1998) and email (75%). Other services and applications, such as purchasing, online sales and advertising/marketing are less extensively used.

The current use of Intranets is low in the UK - about 14% in 1998 (11% in 1997) of companies compared with 32% in Japan and 20% in the USA. Insufficient perceived benefits seems to be a major reason for this low uptake. However, the CMG survey, which was based on a survey of large companies in the UK, found that 48% had an Intranet and these were used mainly for internal communications and knowledge sharing. The introduction was driven mainly by the IT department.

2.6.2 Size of Organisation

It is clear from the DTI (1997) survey that large companies across Europe have higher levels of ownership of hardware and infrastructure than SMEs or very small companies. For example, some 90% of large companies in the UK have access to computers with modems; the figure is 59% for SMEs and 28% for very small companies. For email the figures are 71%, 32% and 16% respectively, for use of the Internet, 47%, 23% and 13% and for the Intranet, 17%, 4% and 0%.

Large and multinational companies are able to adopt new technologies on a global scale, but SMEs and very small companies often lack both the knowledge and resources to invest in ICT effectively. This is borne out by the CyberKix survey which found that 'management policy', 'lack of information on the benefits' of the Internet and 'financial constraints' were the three most important factors preventing SMEs from using the Internet. There is a growing awareness, however, of government initiatives: the 1998 DTI survey found that 63% of UK companies get ICT information from business links, 12% from Chambers of Commerce, 16% from Business Support Organisations and 10% direct from Government Initiatives. The Government's Information Society Initiative is also focused towards smaller companies.

2.6.3 On-line Services: Current Applications

The Internet has spawned a new set of services for advertising, marketing and selling. Primary access to this new environment is by PC, but changing technology may alter this in the future (see section 2.6.4). The 1998 DTI survey found, for example, that 60% of UK businesses had access to the Internet direct from the PC via modem and telephone line, with 25% direct from the PC via ISDN and 18% through a company network. Interestingly, the UK has the second highest Internet access charges behind Germany of the five companies surveyed in the report.

Web sites continue to be the leading environment for online marketing and advertising. In the USA, the 1997 DTI survey found that 39% of all companies and two thirds of large companies had established Web sites. By 1998 the figure had increased to 41% overall. In the UK, in the same year, 27% of all businesses had sites and the figure was 40% for large companies. By 1998 37% of all companies had Web sites in the UK. Advertising and marketing forms the main use (77% to those businesses with access in the UK in 1998) with information distribution (65%), but online sales are limited (13% of businesses).

Most companies, however, are still treating their Web sites as experimental and the majority regard on-line advertising as only 'quite important' or 'not very important' rather than a key marketing component. As Cairncross (op. cit.) pointed out, the Internet will have a very small slice of total advertising revenue well into the first decade of the next century. In 1996 for example, global Internet advertising was $260mn compared with $173bn on all advertising in the USA alone. It is likely that rapid growth will see this change, however.

Indeed, there is a growing distinction between the development of a purely information-based Web site and one which promotes online sales. The former allows a company to inform the customer's buying decision, can help build up market segment information and build a brand presence, whilst the latter can make shopping easier and develop products and services for the electronic environment.

On-line shopping seems likely to develop further. Today, new Web retailers, for example, are cooperating to bring together groups of consumer brands into 'virtual shopping malls'. In France, although consumers already have Minitel (an on-line service based on older technology), this has tended to hold back investment in new ICT, but in the UK many retailers are investing in on-line services, ranging from Tesco, which is looking at on-line ordering of goods for customers, to Aardmarket, which sells branded consumer goods.

However, only 13% of UK businesses in the 1998 DTI survey sold goods on-line (up from 12% in 1997) and only 8% of households have shopped on-line (up from 1% in 1997). Regular NOP surveys suggest, however, that those willing to shop on-line have also doubled in the period 1997-98. Those shopping on the Internet purchase software and hardware, but other products would be also considered, such as books and holidays. Recently the entry of Gap, the well-known high street clothing retailer, was heralded as a sign that 'ecommerce' is about to take off, as security concerns lessen. Traditionally, clothing has been difficult to market and sell on the Internet, but Gap's entry into this field is seen by many as a move to target young, upper-income-level customers and Internet users (Brummer (1998)). Another success story has been the giant online bookstore, Amazon.com.

On-line booking and on-line banking are also growing although they are not yet widespread, despite the introduction of new services. In the UK, for example, only 1% of households have used on-line banking (DTI (1997)). However, the City of London Stock Exchange and its computerised dealing system, SETS, have also parallelled a growth in on-line investing with share prices now readily available on the Internet (Temple (1997)).

Security does appear to be a major issue here: 69% of respondents in the December 1997 NOP survey (DTI (1998)) feared security risks, despite encryption, and 21% felt knowledge and lack of understanding was a barrier to use.

In a related piece of research to the main 1997 DTI survey and its ongoing waves of Internet research, NOP used cluster analysis to categorise the UK Internet user community. They identified six groups ranging in size from 12-24% of users in the UK:

- *Adventurous Team Players*: comprising a quarter of Internet users, they are enthusiastic and have above average business use of the Internet. They are the heaviest users of both the Internet and the Web.

- *Pioneers*: this group is fashion conscious, individualistic and like to stand out in a crowd.

- *Ambivalent Flock*: cautious, and are ambivalent about the Internet - it is neither important nor unimportant to them.

- *Introspective Sceptics*: dislike the Internet, even though some are long-term users.

- *Negative Guides*: tend to find the Internet unenjoyable, unsatisfactory, too slow, difficult to navigate and spoiled by commercialism.

- *Cautious Enthusiasts*: are a contradictory cluster and often operate from academic environments.

Although the Internet is still developing as a commercial tool, NOP research in the period 1996-98 has shown that many more people each year use the Internet. The rate of increase of use by UK adults is rising at 140% for the period 1996-98 with current users at 9 million. The increase in the number of home Web users has outstripped the growth in usage for other localities and is now 28% of all current users.

Furthermore, over half of all businesses using the Internet in the UK are convinced it will radically change the way business is conducted over the next 5 years. Some 72% of all business users, for example, are satisfied with the Internet as a communications medium, and 79% as an information medium. Nevertheless, among those organisations which do not currently have access to the Internet, about two thirds feel they will not gain access to the Internet during the next 12 months.

There is also recent evidence (source: www.nua.ie) that companies do not monitor Web site use effectively: 42% do not monitor the number of visitors and 71% do not monitor the profile or types of people visiting the company. Also only 52% of Web sites are updated only once every 2-3 months, or even less frequently.

2.6.4 Future Developments

The Internet is developing so rapidly that it is difficult to gauge how it will evolve. However, recent innovations in technology suggest that it may be delivered to users by a variety of means and that the distinction between data and voice will blur. NorWeb, for example, have developed Power Line Technology (PLT) using electricity mains transmission to deliver high speed voice and data services over the power distribution network. Internet telephony has also developed to carry voice traffic over the Internet at very low cost, although voice quality is lower than a normal telephone line. Finally, innovations such as Teledesic, which is due to be launched in the USA in 2002, will use satellite technology to provide global Internet connections.

Facts about the Internet

• There were 320 million pages online worldwide in 1998, but this does not include private, encrypted or password-protected documents (source:www.nua.ie)

• There are currently (April 1998) 115.75 million online users in the world, with 70 million in Canada and USA, and 23 million in Europe. For UK the figure is 6 million (or 10.25% of the population). At current rates of growth one billion people may be connected worldwide by 2005. (Source: www.nua.ie and NOP).

• The Internet's pace of adoption has eclipsed all other preceding technologies. Radio was in existence 38 years before 50 million tuned in; TV took 13 years to reach this benchmark, PCs 16 years but the Internet only 4 years. (Source: US Chamber of Commerce (1998): www.ecommerce.gov).

• Internet traffic currently doubles every 100 days. (Source: www.inktomi.com).

• In January 1995, 27,000 top-level commercial (.com) domain names were assigned. In 1997 the figure was 764, 000. (Source: US Chamber of Commerce (1998): www.ecommerce.gov).

• In 1997 $8bn of electronic commerce was transacted on the Web. By 2002 the figure is estimated to be $333bn (source:IDC.com)

2.7 What is the Impact of the Internet on property?

2.7.1 Levels of IT and Internet Use

In comparison with many other sectors of business, and other professions such as accountants, the property profession has often been perceived as being slow to embrace IT. Previous surveys of IT usage (Sullivan (1993) and Dixon (1994)) have revealed relatively low levels of IT penetration and an IT skills gap in the profession. For example, in a 1993/94 survey of individuals at senior management and associate level in GP and QS organisations Dixon (op. cit.) found that many organisations had no IT strategy, and lacked any IT training or education policy. Two sets of factors were found important in promoting the successful introduction of IT:

- intrinsic factors, such as size, type of organisation and maturity of use; and

- 'critical success factors' such as the perception of the importance of IT by an organisation and 'culture'.

More recent evidence, however (Lawson (1997a) and Honey (1997)), suggests that the property industry is finally beginning to take IT on board. Certainly the evidence from Howard (1998) and CICA (1995) suggests the construction industry is using IT in an imaginative and innovative way.

For example, the RICS Members Survey (1997b) found that 80% of members use a computer or word processor and one fifth of these had taken it up within the last two years. Moreover, 30% of computer users currently use external email and 23% the Internet, with levels likely to rise by 20% in each category over the next year. Finally, just over one in three members say their firm/employer has its own Web site, with 25% saying one is planned within the next year.

This means that in 1998, 42% of surveyors should be using the WWW as part of their work and 48% regularly communicating by email. In addition 50% of surveying firms will have an Internet site.

The survey was based on 2309 questionnaires completed from the May 1997 RICS monthly journal CSM. Although they provide a solid base for analysis, the results should be tempered by the twin provisos that they are dependent on respondents reading, completing and returning the questionnaire of their own volition, and that multiple responses from larger organisations may occur.

Finally, the Residential Estate Agency Training and Education Association (REATEA) also carried a survey in the UK in 1997, and found that only 11% of residential estate agents used email and the Internet (REATEA (1997)). In the USA a 1996 similar survey by the National Association of Realtors found that 80% of residential agents with a home page generated about 5% of their business in this way (Weiss (1997)).

The fact remains, however, that we have little detailed information about the use of the Internet and property and are reliant on anecdotal information, which is why the current research is being undertaken.

2.7.2 Using the Internet in the Property Profession

The 'property profession' embraces a wide diversity of work and professional practice. For the purposes of this report the research focuses on the two largest divisions within the RICS, general practice surveying and quantity surveying, and also on corporate organisations such as developers, property companies and financial institutions.

In a general sense, Finch (1996) suggested the Internet offers four main opportunities for the property profession:

- communication;

- research (disseminating and collecting information);

- publishing; and

- marketing.

Each of these activities requires information. Indeed, high quality and relevant information is essential to the profession, but the profession has suffered considerably because of secrecy, confidentiality, and fragmentation of information. The Internet offers important advantages to overcome these problems but requires users to have an understanding of information as a resource. Information is commonly thought of as facts or knowledge gained from study, research or instruction (Doherty (1997)). In the Information Society, however, information can be divided into three categories:

- 'static/archived/reference', which is stable with few changes, making it best suited to storage in a stable, non-fluid environment (eg. print or CD-ROM);

- 'time-dated', such as company brochures, subscription database resources, which require specific periodic updates. This is not as stable as static information and is subject to standardised periodic changes (eg CD-ROM or WWW); and

- 'fluid/kinetic', such as property deals, and construction documents. This type of information changes constantly, and needs to be updated regularly. The Internet is ideally suited to distributing this type of information.

As Doherty (op. cit.:5) points out, *'Information ... knowledge, intelligence, data facts, news, wisdom equals equity. Property professionals create, develop, manage and provide information, and are trained to juggle and filter large amounts of information, to reconcile disparate concepts, and to develop frameworks in which to deliver projects to our clients. Internet technologies are tools (to provide) the opportunity to expand on these skills.'*

How, though, has the Internet developed in the property profession?

Email

At a basic level email has impacted on the profession by enabling communication and collaboration over time and distance, and is currently the most popular application of the Internet amongst property professionals (see Table 2-5). The driving forces for this include clients' increased expectations

Table 2-5 The Current Use of Internet Technology in GP Surveying (source: Honey (1997))

Technology	% use regularly	% use occasionally
Internal email	36	6
External email	17	12
Online Information Services	16	11
WWW	11	13
ISDN	11	3
Intranet	3	2

and demands, as technology and their businesses have advanced, and the expectation of instant information feedback from an easy-to-use medium. There is an economic sense to this also because directly or indirectly the client is paying for redundancy/inefficiency in communications and coordination. Email offers the advantages of lower intrusiveness than the telephone; dealing with multiple emails is easier; keeping records is easier and it is a very cheap form of communication.

Corporate Web Sites

These have also become increasingly common. The RICS (1997a) provides a very useful directory of such Web sites which lists addresses and a brief description of each. As Lawson (1997a) stresses, searching for the term, 'UK Property' on the Internet provides anything from 100,000 to 2.5 million references, and as a sign of the rapid growth in this area, the 1997 Property Computer Show launched 24 new Internet products.

The RICS (1997c) pointed out that surveying firms using Web sites currently fall into three groups:

- small firms where an Internet enthusiast developed the site;
- large or medium-sized firms with professionally developed sites, and
- large firms as part of a 'gateway'.

The reasons for having a Web site also vary from those who see the Internet as a commercial opportunity to those who wish to keep up with or stay ahead of competitors. Examples of the latter two types of site are shown in figures 2-11 and 2-12.

Figure 2-11 Example of Home Page: Jones Lang Wootton

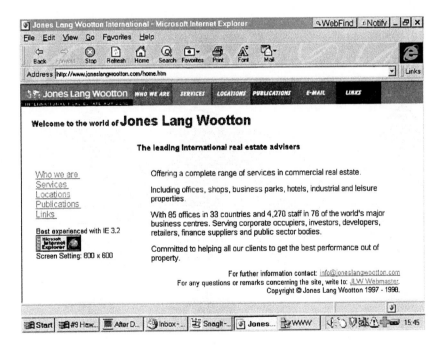

Figure 2-12 Example of Home Page: Property Information Mall

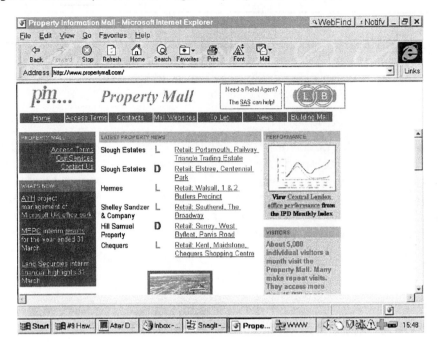

Many of these sites are used to market property as well as the business itself. However, anecdotal evidence suggests no commercial properties have been sold or let on-line (Lawson (op. cit.) and Honey (op. cit.)). Part of the problem appears to lie in the fact that there are too many sites with too few properties. Often sites are badly organised and rarely changed. 'Gateways', or central points for combined listings, have been used with some success. For example, the main London agencies and Estates Gazette have developed PropertyLink, which provides extensive listings of commercial property (www.egpropertylink.co.uk).

The Property Information Mall also offers a structured Internet site for the UK commercial property industry and provides access to news, email addresses, other Web sites and properties (www.propertymall.com).

On-line subscription services

A good example of an on-line subscription service is Focusnet, which is an Internet service provider offering access to a wide range of property data and research via an Intranet. EGi also provides a commercial property news and information service via the Internet as well as a separate property law service, and Focusnet provides Internet access for property professionals, although its main services are delivered through an Intranet (see below). Bridges (1996) provides a useful and extensive coverage of similar sites for construction professionals in the UK, as does Doherty (1997) for sites relevant to both the UK and USA.

Intranet

Examples of Intranets are relatively rare in property. Recently, however, the property and computer press have covered several cases. BT's Intranet, branded as 'Workstyle 2000', includes diary, meeting room facilities and discussion boards. The aim is to improve employees' productivity and time management, and has already resulted in savings of £600 million per year in internal mail, couriers and employees' time (Tinworth (1997)). This has taken place against the backdrop of the re-engineering of the whole office and even CV details of work experience are included so that others in the company can find the expert they need.

Property Intelligence's Focus services are also currently provided under an Intranet umbrella. Property Focus, for example, contains 250,000 records on commercial property across the UK, and there are a range of other subscription services such as Town and Country Focus, and Relocation Focus.

2.7.3 What are the implications of the Internet for the property profession?

The Internet is likely to impact in two main ways:

- work practices and organisational structures, and

- property market and occupier/client requirements.

Work Practices and Organisational Structures

In terms of work practices, for example, email provides much easier collaboration and access to sources of expertise which might not otherwise be available. It can also flatten organisations, removing their hierarchical structure, and enable more effective project team-based work. Edkins (1997) for example, shows how in a typically fragmented UK construction industry the Internet and email can improve project team coordination in terms of linking the client, design consultants, the quantity surveyor, project manager, main contractor and specialist sub-contractor. Doherty (1997) lists the advantages of such an approach:

- facilitates assembling, managing and operating construction project teams;

- removes the time/place barriers between collaborating members;

- allows managers to assemble teams by tapping into people; and

- creates smaller interdisciplinary teams.

Email enables construction practices to uncover hidden expertise by providing better coverage than the telephone. Expertise on a global scale around the clock can be accessed and smaller companies also benefit from reduced isolation and the opportunity to collaborate. Disadvantages include the time spent on email use by employees and, related to this, excessive volumes of email, including 'spamming' or junk email. A 1998 survey by Novell/Benchmark Research (sourced at www.nua.ie), for example, found that junk mail could be costing British and Irish businesses up to $8.2 billion per year. Some 75% of respondents stated they received up to 5 junk emails per day.

In commercial agency work, the wider access to property information on the Internet has implications for the traditional role of the surveyor as 'information broker'. For example, organisations are now using the Internet to market their own properties, making a shift in emphasis for the surveyor towards 'interpreter and filterer' of readily available information more likely (Haddock (1995), Wyatt (1996) and Davis (1997)). The term 'disintermediation' has been coined (Tapscott (1997)), to represent the elimination of middleman functions between producers and consumers through the use of digital networks. This means middle businesses, functions and people need to move up the business chain to create new value. Tapscott uses the example of real estate brokers in the USA and Canada who match property owners with buyers or lessees. They are intermediaries acting on behalf of the property owner and they work as part of a team to put the deal together. As critical information becomes more readily available, the intermediaries come under threat. Tapscott quotes an Ontario broker:

'As technology facilitates the exchange of information between suppliers and customers, we need to find new ways to deliver value to our clients. Rather than being in the transaction or information exchange business we need to become value-added facilitators of deals and ongoing partners for commercial real estate advice, and knowledge and help. In doing so, it will make more sense for sellers to partner with us rather than to try and do it themselves.'

For example, when leasing space in a new shopping centre the broker needs to understand not only the customer and the potential purchaser but also the customers' customers in terms of demography, local population, employment levels and so on.

In the USA, deal and transactions data is more readily and openly available than it is in England and Wales, where secrecy and confidentiality of property information is still a real issue (SPR (1995). Despite initiatives such as the National Land Information system (NLIS), which evolved from the RICS Domesday 2000 project, moving us closer in this country towards a fully integrated national land and property information system, progress is still therefore slow. Rowley, Fisher and Holmes (1998) have also suggested a National Valuation Evidence Database (NVED) as a way of enabling surveying practices to pool data. The multiplicity of data platforms and lack of consistency in such simple standards as address makes this difficult to achieve in the short term, but as more data is opened up it may be that the surveyor's role will shift in emphasis to one of adding value through expert interpretation as is happening in the USA.

A similar pattern is occurring in construction with the emergence of what Doherty (1997) calls 'Construction Information Managers': professionals who are comfortable with IT and can visualise its value for business, yet are also adept at facilitating and transferring valuable information to clients.

The need to collaborate with other experts in multidisciplinary teams has also led to what Doherty (op. cit.) calls 'coopetition', or the making of limited scope agreements and contacts with an organisation's traditional competition. The global nature of the Internet has created a much wider diversity of available clients and competitive market 'cooperative local partners', allied to our organisation, can assist in fighting off competition.

This competition is in fact partly generated from other professions such as accountants, specialist management consultants, and other institutional advisers. Very often such organisations already have a track record in using the Internet to generate business: indeed comparison with these groups can serve as a useful benchmark. The savings market is being transformed by IT for example (Ginarlis (1997)).

National Land Information System (NLIS)

The NLIS concept evolved in England and Wales from the Citizen's Charter White Paper of 1992 and seeks to provide a service to allow access via IT to geographically-related information from a number of sources. In essence the aim is to provide a one-stop shop for land and property information. SCOTLIS is the Scottish equivalent.

In April 1998 a conveyancing pilot exercise went live in Bristol. Linking twelve data providers, the pilot uses an index, and a land and property gazetteer, based on BS7666. Searches can be made by solicitors to twelve data providers, including the City Council, Land Registry, Land Charges Department, Coal Authority and Valuation Office. The system is map-based and is accessed via the Web.

(source: www.nlis.org.uk)

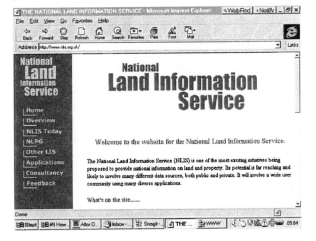

Visions of the Future: Cyberplaces?

Forecasting future trends in technology is always extremely risky. To many people the idea of a workable, 3D, virtual environment (or simulated reality) is a pipe-dream or something out of Science Fiction. Yet the idea of 'cyberplaces' is a reality. Based on the concept of 'cyberspace', a term coined by William Gibson in his 1984 novel, 'Neuromancer' which describes the world of computers and society that surrounds them, cyberplaces are sites in cyberspace where information can be obtained and shared, skills learned and practised and virtual environments created.

The construction industry is particularly suited to this development, and a good example is the Collaborative Integrated Communications for Construction (CICC) project based in the UK. The project is looking at alternative Web-based virtual reality interfaced to support intuitive navigation and how project information is accessed and presented. Open Internet and Intranet networks are used to provide information to the project team, and browser software is used to provide the client, consultant, contractor, subcontractors and suppliers with remote office or construction site access to team members and project information.

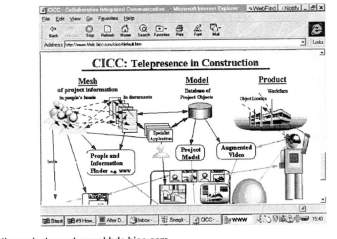

More details on the project are at www.hhdc.bicc.com.

Property Market and Occupier/Client Requirements

The Internet is beginning to affect clients and occupiers' property requirements. The declining influence of distance through the use of Internet technology has meant that traditional patterns of employment and the associated office and retail locations have come under threat. Trends towards 'teleworking', or working at home with an electronic office link, have emerged and on-line shopping has been introduced by a number of retailers. Views as to how substantial these trends are and when they will impact differ, however. As Arthur C. Clarke pointed out, people often exaggerate the short run impacts of technological change and underestimate the long run impacts.

A recent survey by the University of Reading (1997) assessed the extent to which changing work practices and business organisation affect demand for business space, and the implications for property market practice. Globalisation, innovation in ICT, reorganisation of working practices and the drive for flexibility were changes which would have important implications for the demand for business space and the functioning of property markets. However, the research, which was based on a survey of business occupiers and focus groups, found that although changes in business organisations and new work practices were leading to a decrease in demand for space, the decline in aggregate demand is not great. This stems partly from the fact that new practices such as teleworking and homeworking have only recently had an effect on small numbers of employees, and partly from the fact that new sources of demand from outsourcing (or separating certain administrative functions), are arising elsewhere. For example, 87% or firms had outsourced some of their business activities, but in the majority of cases less than 5% of staff were affected. A key driver or enabler of change is IT, but without IT other management and organisation changes are not possible. The overall impression gained is of slow change and only limited impact on the requirement for business space: although change is likely to occur it will be gradual rather than sudden, the report concluded.

Markham (1998) supports this view in relation to the future of shopping centres. Although other commentators argue that on-line shopping will create surplus retail space, Markham argues that retail, catalogue and on-line sales can all exist side-by-side. Pointing to the relatively low current levels of on-line shopping he believes (op. cit.: 28-9): '... the amount of traditional retail space required will still be substantial. If there is a fall out of space it is likely to be felt in secondary locations and tend to reinforce the premium value of the best areas. ...Cyberspace could, on my scenario, benefit property.' As much as anything, the psychological needs of concentrated retail shoppers will, in Markham's opinion, mean any impact from the Internet is gradual and limited. These views are also confirmed by anecdotal evidence collected by Lawson (1997b). Despite the fact that 'ecommerce' is taking off, online sales are likely to supplement rather than replace 'traditional' shopping. In the next decade, however, there may be a drive towards shorter leases, and greater availability of multi-purpose buildings, for example.

The future is uncertain, but it is clear that the Internet will have an impact on property and client requirements: consensus suggests this is unlikely to be over the short term. However, on a national scale new technology will have an increasing impact in the long term; as Cairncross (op. cit.: 234) puts it:

'The death of distance will shape the world of the mid twenty-first century more profoundly than the world of the next decade.'

2.8 Summary and Conclusions

The literature review has highlighted the importance of a number of key issues:

- The importance of the Internet as a marketing tool. Its phenomenal growth, founded on email and more recently the World Wide Web, will, in the opinion of many experts, change the nature of business and commerce. Companies are also introducing Intranets as they see the benefits of a Web-based interface for data and communications within their own organisations.

- Research by the DTI has shown, however, that barriers operate to constrain the growth of the Internet and other forms of ICT. Often a failure of SMEs to understand and appreciate the new technology is at the heart of these constraints. In short, previous surveys suggest SMEs may lack the knowledge and resources to invest in ICT effectively.

- Weaving the Internet into an organisation's IT strategy also seems to be an important element. McBride's (op cit) framework, for example, offers a useful summary of how the levels of Internet dependency can vary within business, and Doherty (op cit) shows how a design and construction business can evolve from a 'computer-aided' business to one where active information sharing with clients occurs.

- Despite its advantages, commentators such as Frances Cairncross see the Internet as having only a limited impact on advertising revenue in the short term. It is likely that on-line shopping and banking will develop further, however, over the medium term.

- In comparison with other sectors of business, very little research has been carried out into the impact of the Internet on the property profession. Previous surveys of IT have indicated low levels of IT usage, but a recent RICS survey found higher levels of IT use, including email (Honey, op cit). Some (Tapscott (op cit)) have argued that 'disintermediation' may result in professional work as buyers and sellers are bought closer together. Changes in organisational structures may also occur as the Internet and other technologies gain a foothold. Research by the University of Reading has shown that changes in work practice in client and occupiers' organisations are having only a limited impact on space requirements.

New research is therefore needed to provide a detailed study which reviews the impact of the Internet on the property profession. The current research has been developed to provide:

- an up-to-date survey on the usage and attitudes of surveyors towards the Internet and related technology, including Intranets;

- a clearer view of the 'critical success factors' (or 'drivers') which operate in enabling professional surveying practices or varying size to introduce and use the Internet in the most efficient and effective ways;

- a better understanding of the 'barriers' to the successful introduction of the Internet and how they may be overcome;

- a better understanding of the key benefits for organisations using the Internet; and

- a better understanding of the Internet and its current and future impact on professional work, operational practice and property/client requirements.

3. METHODOLOGY

3.1 Introduction

This chapter of the report describes the methodology used for the current research and the basis for identifying the sample.

The research was based on an extensive postal questionnaire survey of 671 surveying practices and corporate organisations carried out in March 1998 and this was followed up by eight detailed case study interviews in May 1998.

3.2 Identification of the Survey Sample

The two largest divisions within the RICS are the General Practice and Quantity Surveying divisions, comprising some 44.8% and 34.6% of total members respectively (RICS (1997d)). Corporates, or commercial concerns, are also important, however. Irrespective of division, 21% of members work for property companies, financial institutions and other similar organisations (the corporates figure for private practice surveying firms is some 55%).

Although there are seven professional divisions within the RICS it was decided to focus on three main groups as being the most important:

- general practice surveying firms;
- quantity surveying firms, and
- corporates (such as corporate property owners, property companies, financial institutions and developers).

From this it was intended that the lessons and findings from the research would also be of relevance to other divisions and functional specialisms within the RICS: for example, commercial property, residential property and construction.

Size of organisation was also an issue to consider. The RICS database, which provided the basis for the sample of organisations, allows a sampling frame to be constructed on the basis of the number of partners with each firm. Figure 3-1 and Table 3-1 show the relative size distribution of GP and QS firms in 1998. Unfortunately, no comparative information exists for corporates.

To enable comparisons to be made more easily between the three groups according to their size, disproportionate stratified random sampling was used. This involves 'stratification' or segregation, into various groups which are not proportional to their numbers in the population as a whole, followed by a random selection of subjects from each stratum. This should ensure that there is more 'between-group' differences than 'within-group' differences and sampling on this basis avoids the potential problem of low numbers in a stratum.

The overall size of each institution within the frame groups was, of course, constrained by the maximum number of firms available. Table 3-2 shows the details of the sample. In all, 671 firms were selected as the basis for the postal questionnaire survey.

Figure 3-1 Size Distribution for GP and QS Firms: 1998 (source:RICS)

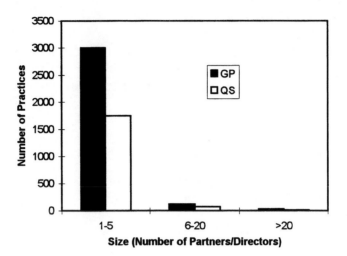

Table 3-1 RICS Member Organisations by Size and Type (source:RICS)

	1-5	6-20	>20	Total
General Practice	3004	116	31	3151
Quantity Surveying`	1749	71	14	1834
Corporates	n/a	n/a	n/a	n/a

These size categories were chosen because of the spread of actual frequencies within GP and QS firms. Table 3-1 shows that three types of size category were chosen:
- 1-5 partners/directors ('small');
- 6-20 partners/directors ('medium/large'); and,
- >20 partners/directors ('very large').

As Table 3-1 shows, adopting a proportionate sample would have skewed responses towards smaller organisations and made valid comparison difficult.

Table 3-2 Sample Details - Number of Organisations by Size and Type

	Number of Partners/Directors			
	1-5	6-20	>20	Total
General Practice	118	116*	31*	265
Quantity Surveying	118	71*	14*	203
Corporates	n/a	n/a	n/a	203

* =Maximum available from RICS dataset

3.3 Research Design

3.3.1 Postal Questionnaire

The questionnaire, which is shown in Appendix 1, was sent to named senior partners or directors where possible in each type of organisation. Where no name was available the questionnaire was mailed to the senior partner in charge of IT, or the IT manager, in the case of GP and QS firms, and the Senior Director or the IT manager in the case of corporates.

The questionnaire covered the following areas:

- the organisation, including size and geographic distribution;
- PCs and networking, including the presence of a formal IT strategy and the use (or otherwise) of IT;
- the Internet, including:
    - the use of email and why it was introduced;
    - the use of the Web;
    - the driving forces for implementing the Internet and Intranets;
    - the barriers to Internet use;
    - whether the organisation has a Web page, and when it was set up;
    - what the important benefits are from introducing the Internet.
- Intranet use (if any) in the organisation;
- views on the future of the Internet and its impact on property.

To maximise the response, a reminder letter was sent 10 days after the original despatch of the questionnaire, and a short telephone survey conducted to investigate non-response bias (see section 4.2).

3.3.2 Case Study Interviews

The questionnaire included a question as to whether the respondent would be willing to be involved in a case study interview for the research. After the results to this question were analysed, eight case studies interviews were initiated, which comprised:

- medium-sized GP practice (two);
- very large international surveying practice (two);
- medium/large GP practice;
- large international surveying practice;
- large QS practice; and
- large property company.

In each case structured, taped interviews were carried out which covered the following areas:

- the evolution of the Internet in the practice;
- the development of the home page;
- using the Internet and its impact on professional work;
- the critical success factors for its introduction;
- future development of the Internet in the organisation.

A lack of positive response to the question on interviews from small organisations meant that the case studies concentrated on medium sized and larger organisations. Nonetheless the lessons learned from these case studies and the postal questionnaire are applicable to small organisations.

3.3.3 Statistical Testing

Limited statistical testing was carried out to explore the following hypotheses:

1. Email access is associated with the size and type of organisation.

2. Web access is associated with the size and type of organisation.

3. Intranet access is associated with the size and type of organisation.

4. The relative importance of 'barriers' to the Internet varies according to the size and type of organisation and whether it has Web access.

5. The relative importance of 'benefits' to the Internet varies according to the size and type of organisation.

6. The relative importance of 'drivers' for the Internet varies according to the size and type of organisation.

Hypotheses 1 to 3 were tested using Chi-Square Tests and Hypotheses 4 to 6 with Kruskal-Wallis tests.

4. RESULTS: QUESTIONNAIRE AND CASE STUDIES

4.1 Introduction

This chapter presents the results of the research in three main sections:

- sample and response rates;
- postal questionnaire results;
- case study interviews.

Each section provides a summary and overview of the results. A copy of the questionnaire is provided in Appendix 1. The full results, broken down by type of organisation and size, are given in Appendix 2 in the yellow pages at the end of the report.

Limited statistical testing was also carried out and the results are given in section 4.3.8.

4.2 Questionnaire Sample, Size of Organisation and Response Rates

The postal questionnaire was sent to 671 firms and a total of 261 responses were received, which is a 39% overall response rate. The response by type and size of organisation is shown in Table 4-1.

Table 4-1 Response Rate by Type and Size of Organisation

Type	Responses	Sent	Response Rate
GP	125	265	47%
QS	84	203	41.4%
Corporates	52	203	25.6%

Size	1-5	6-20	20>
GP	59.3%	24.1%	87%
QS	53.3%	21.2%	42.8%
Corporates	n/a	n/a	n/a

The size categories in Table 4-1 are represented by:

- 1-5 partners/directors ('small');
- 6-20 partners/directors ('medium/large'); and,
- >20 partners/directors ('very large').

These categories are consistent with the sampling frame adopted and are supported by the break points in size categories within the responses received. They also enable a simpler presentation of results. Where question 1.4 (number of partners) was not completed, a judgement on the size of organisation was made on the basis of response to question 1.5 (number of employees) and 1.6 (geographical distribution). This applied particularly to corporates.

It should also be noted that although the sampling frame adopted in this research is able to show differences between size categories more easily, the actual population of both GP and QS practices contains proportionately larger numbers of sole practitioners and small businesses (see Tables 3-1 and 3-2) than the sample itself.

Figure 4-1 Sample by Organisation Type

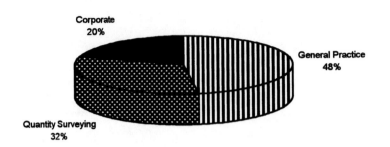

Figure 4-1 shows the breakdown of the sample by organisation type. Although the overall response rate was good, some 61% of respondents did not respond, and there may be particular reasons for this, which might cause bias in the results. For example, a much larger percentage of non-respondents than respondents may not use PCs, email or the Web.

To find out more about the characteristics of the non-respondents we carried out a short telephone survey of 80 non-respondents from the 1-5 and 6-20 categories for the GP and QS groups. Interviewees were asked whether they had PCs, email and Internet access. The comparative results are shown in Table A1 of Appendix 2. Although there are some differences between the respondents and non-respondents (particularly in the 1-5 size category) these are relatively small, so we can be confident that the effect of non-response bias is minimal.

Generally speaking, the questionnaire reached the appropriate senior person in the organisation, as Table B2 in Appendix B shows. Senior management dominated the responses, therefore, with more than 43% of the sample being at senior partner/partner or director level. The 'other' category included titles such as 'head of research', 'chairman' and 'company secretary'.

Tables B1 to B7 give further information on the characteristics of the sample, including number of employees, geographic distribution, RICS market areas.

Table B8 shows whether organisations had a separate IT department or IT support. Although 37.5% do have a separate IT department, 62.5% do not. This is particularly interesting to analyse as the size and type of organisation appears to affect the response. Table B9 shows that as size of organisation increases, a separate IT department or IT support is more common, and corporates and GP practices are more likely to have a separate IT function than QS practices (Table B10).

The results that are presented are unweighted, but it should be appreciated that, as Table 3-2 showed, the population of GP and QS practices contains a high number of 'small' practices. The lack of information about size categories in the corporates group and the differences in response rate between the GP and QS groups are both valid reasons for doing this. For comparative purposes, however, the unweighted and weighted results are given in Table A2 of Appendix 2 (see also sections 3.2 and 5.3.1).

4.3 Questionnaire Results

4.3.1 PCs and Networking

Some 53% of the sample had a formal IT strategy (Table B11), but this was more common in corporates (78.4%) than in QS (50%) and GP (45.2%). Size of organisations also appeared to be an important factor. Table B13 in Appendix 2 shows that 92.6% of very large GP and 100% of very large QS practices had a formal IT strategy whereas the figures were 20.3% and 34.9% respectively for small and medium/large organisations.

Laptops and mobiles were common in corporate organisations and in larger organisations generally (figure 4-2 and Tables B16 to B18). Indeed, 96.9% of the sample had at least some form of PC (figure 4-3 and Table B14). Only 8

Figure 4-2 Type of PC by Organisation Type

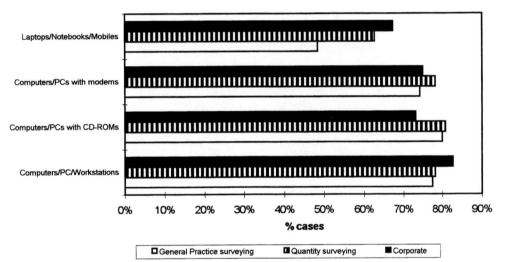

Figure 4-3 Presence of PCs

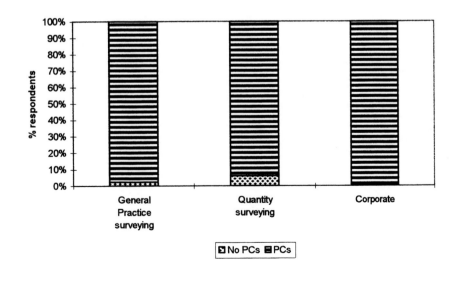

respondents (3.1%) did not have any PC. (The most important reasons being 'no need' and 'need to know more about IT' -Table B19)).

The majority of respondent organisations were also networked (65.6%) and, again, larger numbers of corporates and large organisations tend to be networked (Tables B20 to B22). Indeed, only 7.7% of corporates were not networked. The reasons for not networking, which applied to larger proportions of GP (38%) and QS (45.8%) were dominated by the fact that there was 'only one PC' (42.4%) - Table B23 - and that there was 'no need for networking' (38.8%) - see figure 4-4. Breakdown by type and size of organisation is shown in Tables B24 and B25.

Figure 4-4 Reasons for Not Networking

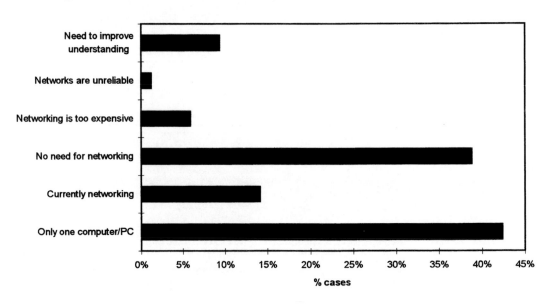

4.3.2 The Internet

Email

Email is used by 68.9% of respondents (see figure 4-5), and 19.2% have at least plans to use it in the short to long term (Table B26). More corporates (76.9%) use email than GP (64.8%) and QS (70.3%) and larger organisations of all types use email more than smaller organisations (Tables B26 to B28). For example, 48.5% of small GP practices compared with 100% of very large GP practices.

The primary use of email appears to be for 'communication with customers/clients' (81.7% of all cases), and this is shown in figure 4.6 and Table B29. This is also true when broken down by type of organisation (81.7%, 90.5% and 68.3% for GP, QS and corporates respectively), and by size, except for very large corporates, where 'communication with others' (69.2%) receives the highest percentage. The figures are shown in Tables B29 to B31.

In terms of the reasons for introducing email, the most important reason overall (a median and mode rank of 1) was to increase efficiency (figure 4.7 and Table B32). This was also the most important reason for each type and size of organisation. (Tables B33 to B37).

Figure 4-5 Use of Email

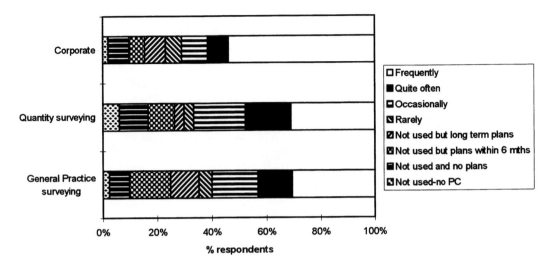

Figure 4-6 Reasons for Email use

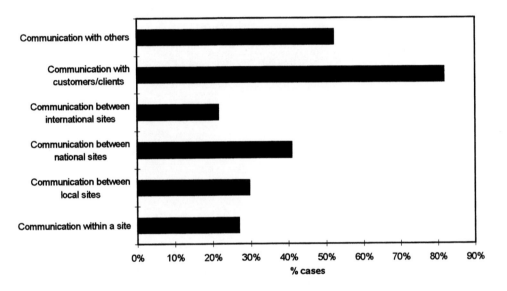

Figure 4-7 Reasons for Introducing Email

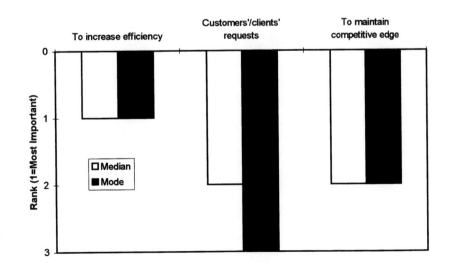

4.3.3 World Wide Web (WWW)

As figure 4-8 shows, 56.3% of respondent organisations had access to the World Wide Web, and a further 10% had no current access but were seeking to gain access in the short term (i.e. 6 months). Corporates were generally more likely to have access (71.2%) than GP (52.8%) and QS (52.4%). Larger organisations of all three groups were also more likely to have access than smaller ones. For example, 64.2% of medium/large GP firms had access, but only 37.1% of small GP firms. The figures for small and medium/large corporates were 83% and 64.7% respectively. The full details are provided in Tables B35 to B37.

Figure 4-8 Access to World Wide Web

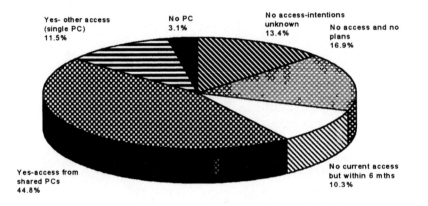

Figure 4-9 shows that 'research' (74.3% of cases) is the single most important use of Internet and WWW. This was also the case for all three types of organisation (71.8%, 83% and 69% for GP, QS and Corporates respectively). However, when the other types of use are examined, the importance varies: the next most important use is 'news' for GP, 'business contacts' for QS and 'market trends' for corporates. 'Advertising/marketing' the business and property 'marketing/comparables' were less important (40.7% and 25.1% respectively) although for GP the figures were higher (48.7% and 33.3%). Tables B38 to B40 give the details.

Figure 4-9 Use of World Wide Web

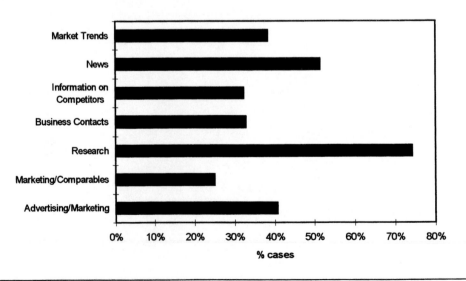

Access to the Internet was controlled with a formal policy by only 35% respondent organisations with PCs. Greater numbers of respon[dent] organisations in corporate organisations had a formal Internet policy (49%) than the two other groups and an access policy was more common in larger organisations. All large QS practices had Internet access policies compared with only 20.8% of small QS practices. Details are given in Tables B41 to B43.

The main driving force for the development of the Internet course comes from the IT department for organisations as a whole (40.7%). However, for GP firms the 'other' category was most important, and particularly amongst smaller firms where the sole practitioner or principal was a key driving force. In other instances, the research or accounts department had played a key role and these categories in fact dominated the 'other' group. Tables B44 to B46 give the full details.

Overall, 34% of organisations had a home page on the World Wide Web. The figure amongst corporates was highest (46.2%), compared with 33.6% GP and 26.6% QS (see figure 4-10) organisations. As organisations increased in size the numbers with a home page also increased (see Tables B47 to B49). For example, 20.9% of small QS firms, compared with 50% of very large.

The mean number of hits on the home page was 4472 per month. But the range of figures given are very variable, from a minimum of 10 to a maximum of 80,000. Corporates had the highest number of visits (7956 per month) compared with GP (4849) and QS (324). Details are given in Table B50.

The most popular Internet Service Provider was Demon with 19% of responses, followed by Compuserve (11.8%), Pipex (9.2%) and Focusnet (5.9%). Focusnet was uniquely used by 10.7% of GP firms, which was the second highest group behind Demon (20%) in the group. Details are given in Tables B51 to B52.

Figure 4-10 Presence of Web Site by Organisation Type

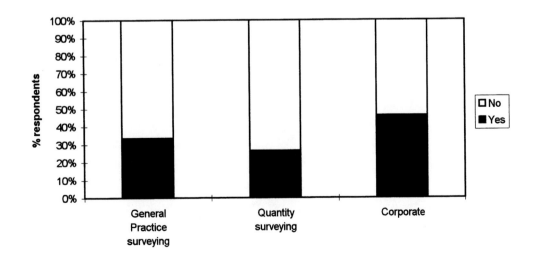

Finally, the pattern of home page growth in the profession is shown quite clearly in figure 4-11. The years 1996 and 1997 showed a particularly rapid period of growth as has the first part of 1998 with 14 new sites. A similar pattern emerges for all types of organisation. Tables B55 to B54 shows the pattern in detail.

Figure 4-11 Growth of Web Sites by Organisation Type

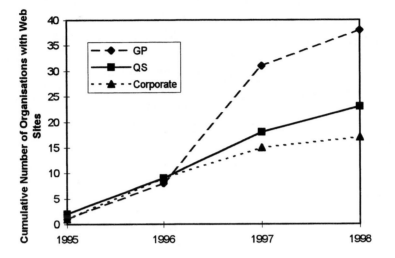

4.3.4 Intranets

Overall, only 16.9% of respondents had Intranet facilities. Corporates (44%) are much more likely to have Intranet facilities than either GP (12.8%) or QS (6%) organisations. But larger GP and QS firms are more likely to have Intranets than smaller firms. See figure 4-12 and Tables B55 to B57.

Figure 4-12 Presence of Intranets by Organisation Type

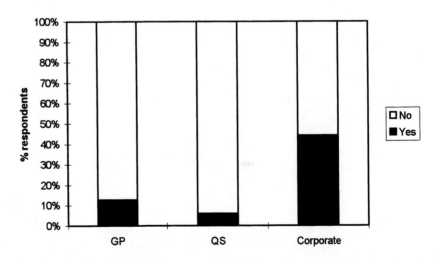

Organisations are most likely to use Intranets for 'company information' (80.9% of cases with Intranets) and 'email' (66% of cases with Intranets), as shown in figure 4-13. This is apparent across all three types of organisation, and is also clear from Tables B58 to B60.

Figure 4-13 Use of Intranets

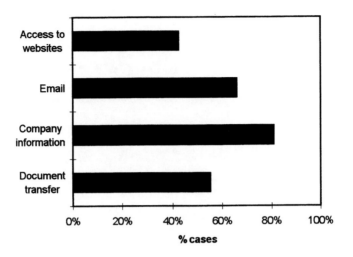

Internationally networked offices comprised 23.3% of respondents with Intranets, but usually (60.5%) the linkage was within the UK. International networks were commonest in the GP and corporate groups and size was again an important factor. Some 22% of large GP firms were networked internationally, for example. Tables B61 to B63 shows the full picture.

Again, the pattern of Intranet growth mirrors that of Web growth with substantial take off in intranets occurring in 1997 (see figure 4-14), as shown in Tables B64 and B65.

Figure 4-14 Growth of Intranets

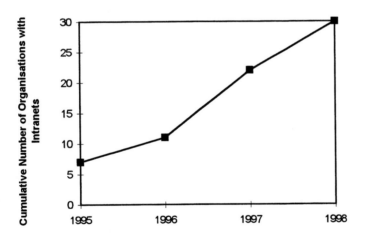

The main driving force for Intranet growth has again been the IT department, in 68.3% of organisations overall. The same is true of GP, QS and Corporates as is shown in Tables B65 to B67.

4.3.5 *Barriers, Benefits and Drivers of the Internet/Intranet*

Barriers to the Internet
Respondents were asked how important certain barriers are to the use of the Internet in the organisation. Figure 4-15 shows the results. 'Lack of security'

Figure 4-15 Barriers to Internet

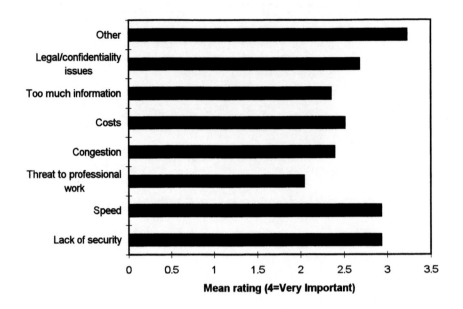

(a mean rating of 2.93) and 'speed' (also 2.93) and 'legal/confidentiality issues' (2.68) were the three most important barriers overall. The 'other' category was also important. Table 4.2 below shows a selection of the responses to this, which generally related to 'time-consuming' or 'time-wasting' through information searches.

Table 4-2 'Other' Barriers

'lack of structure'	*'lack of robustness'*
'staff time consuming'	*'lack of property related features'*
'competing with larger firms'	*'time to organise'*
'time consuming'	*'relevance'*
'technical - still learning'	*'time wasting'*
'too much useless information'	*'time'*
'inappropriate use by staff'	

There are differences between the three types of organisation, and by size, as Tables B69 and B70 show, but 'lack of security' and 'speed' are ranked at least in the top three factors for each type of organisation.

Interestingly, breaking down the importance of barriers by whether organisations have Web access or not reveals some differences (figure 4-16 and Table B71). For those with Web access the top three factors are 'speed', 'lack of security' and 'legal/confidentiality' issues, but for those without Web access 'legal/confidentiality', 'lack of security' and 'costs' are important (although 'speed' is also close to costs). The full results are shown in Tables B68 to B71.

Figure 4-16 Barriers to Internet Use

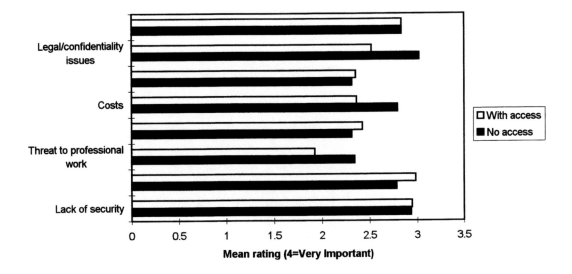

Benefits of the Internet

Figure 4-17 shows that the most important benefit for organisations overall is 'increased competitive advantage' (a rating of 3.10). This is closely followed by 'reduced communication costs' (2.83) and the 'reduced cost of sharing information' (3.0). Organisational differences occur, but 'increased competitive advantage is still important across all three types of organisation. The full results by type and size of organisation are shown in Tables B72 and B74.

Figure 4-17 Benefits of Internet

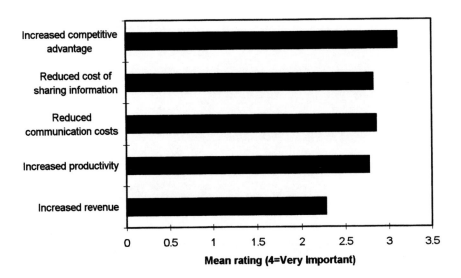

Drivers for Internet/Intranets

The three most important drivers promoting Internet and Intranet use are 'senior management support' (figure 4-18) (a rating of 3.03), 'existing IT culture' (2.71) and 'involvement of all staff' (2.42). 'Linkage to the business plan' (2.21) is considered relatively unimportant, although the differences between these factors are quite small.

Organisational differences also occur after the top two factors, which are 'senior management support' and 'existing IT culture', across all three types of organisation. Interestingly, QS and corporates rate a 'formal IT strategy' as being the third most important factor, but the GP group rate 'involvement of all staff' as the third most important factor. The full range of results is given in Tables B75 to B77.

Figure 4-18 Drivers for Internet/Intranets

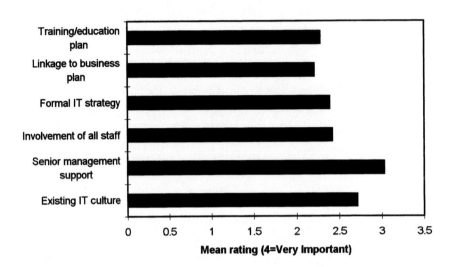

4.3.6 The Impact of the Internet on the Surveying Profession

There were clear views as to the truth of the statements:

- 'The Internet will replace the surveyor's role as information broker';
- 'The Internet will soon impact on the location and occupancy of our clients' businesses', and
- 'Surveyors must understand and use the Internet to maintain their competitive advantage'.

The first two statements received low scores overall but there was stronger agreement with the third (figure 4-19), which suggests that although

Figure 4-19 Attitudes to the Impact of the Internet

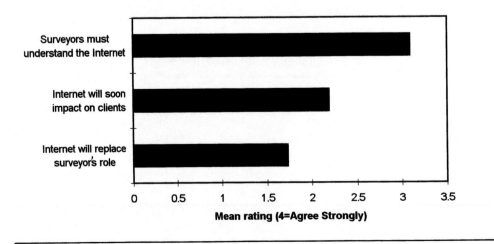

surveyors are protective of their competitive advantage they do not see the Internet as a threat to their traditional role. When organisation types are compared, a similar pattern emerges, although corporates give a slightly higher rating (2.02) to the replacement of the surveyor's role statement than other organisations (GP, 1.70 and QS, 1.59). The full results are shown in Tables B78 to B80.

4.3.7 Other Issues

Question 4.3 on the postal questionnaire invited comments from respondents. These are shown in full in Appendix 3 - a number of themes emerged from these comments:

Uses

- email is a particular benefit of Internet access;

- the use of the Internet as a property marketing tool is still limited, but it is valuable for accessing and transferring information;

Problems

- there is a marked resistance to the use of the Internet and IT generally amongst older, senior professionals;

- time-wasting can be a problem, particularly when searching for information on the Web;

- smaller firms (particularly sole practitioners) often cannot see an advantage in using the Internet because of the way they do business through personal contact;

The Future

- there needs to be more property-related information available on the Web that can be accessed easily;

- surveyors' skills will still be needed for interpretation of information so that professional services are not directly under threat in the short term;

- the RICS should offer more advice and information on how the Internet can benefit the property profession.

4.3.8 Statistical Testing

As size and type of organisation appeared to be key factors in explaining differences to response in the questionnaire, some limited, non-parametric statistical tests were carried out.

The following hypotheses were tested:

1. Email access is associated with the size and type of organisation.

2. Web access is associated with the size and type of organisation.

3. Intranet access is associated with the size and type of organisation.

4. The relative importance of 'barriers' to the Internet varies according to the size and type of organisation, and whether it has Web access.

5. The relative importance of 'benefits' to the Internet varies according to the size and type of organisation.

6. The relative importance of 'drivers' for the Internet varies according to the size and type of organisation.

Hypotheses 1 to 3 were tested using Chi-Square Tests and Hypotheses 4 to 6 with Kruskal-Wallis tests.

Email Access and Web Access

The statistical tests indicated that size is a more important factor in explaining email and Web access than type of organisation. Table 4-3 gives the results with the shaded cells showing results that are significant at the 5% level. This means that the greater the size of organisation (of whatever type) the more likely it is to have email, Web and Intranet access. It also means that larger corporate organisations are more likely to have Intranet access than other groups.

Table 4-3 Chi-Square Results for Hypotheses 1 and 2

Independent Variable	Dependent Variable	Chi-Square	Significance
Size	Email access	28.19	<.001
Type	Email access	2.67	0.263
Size	Web access	23.20	<.001
Type	Web access	4.63	0.099
Size	Intranet access	73.44	<.001
Type	Intranet access	40.14	<.001

Barriers, Benefits, and Drivers

Table 4-4 gives only those factors that were significant at the 5% level. There was therefore no 'benefit' that differed significantly between size or type of organisation.

Table 4-4 Kruskal-Wallis Results for Hypotheses 3 and 5

Independent Variable	Dependent Variable	Chi-square	Significance
	Barriers		
Size	Lack of security	9.79	.007
Type	Lack of security	7.644	.022
Type	Legal/ Confidentiality	5.816	.05
Web access	Threat to professional work	5.27	.022
Web access	Costs	7.329	.007
Web access	Legal/ Confidentiality	9.145	.002
	Drivers		
Size	Existing IT Culture	6.39	.041
Size	Formal IT strategy	23.86	<.001
Type	Formal IT strategy	6.07	.048

As regards 'barriers', larger organisations rated 'lack of security' most important and this was significant at the 5% level. Again, corporates rated 'lack of security' and 'legal/confidentiality' issues higher than the two other groups and this was significant at the 5% level. Finally, organisations without Web access rated 'threats to professional work', 'costs' and 'legal/confidentiality' issues more of a barrier than those with Web access.

For 'drivers', size was a significant factor in explaining differences in the score for 'existing IT culture' and 'formal IT strategy'. Larger organisations rated these factors more important than smaller ones. Finally, corporates rated 'formal IT strategy' as a driver more highly than GP and QS groups.

4.4 Case Studies

The details of the eight case studies are provided in Appendix 4. This section of the report is based on the headings of the structured interviews and gives selected quotes to support the points made.

4.4.1 Evolution of the Internet

In larger organisations email access and a Web presence has often been pre-dated by an existing internal office computer network. In some cases the driving force has been the IT department, but in organisations where there is no IT department, others, such as Head of Research (a medium-sized GP practice in the group of eight (Case Study 1)), or Information Services (a corporate case study (Case Study 8) in the group of eight) have taken responsibility. Several organisations, however, saw no need for an internal IT department, and these were not just small organisations. As one senior partner put it:

> 'A firm like us doesn't have the time to fiddle around internally resourcing an IT department or shopping around for people to guide us. We expect it of our consultants.' Senior Partner (GP)

In the case of one QS firm other related issues had proved a problem when dealing with projects with different data interchange formats.

> 'Nearly every new project of any size now comes with its own electronic communications system like PIMS or Hummingbird, or BT Construct and we have to cope with these different systems.' IT Manager (QS)

4.4.2 Home Page

All the interviewees said their home pages had been developed over the last 2-3 years. Responsibility for development followed the pattern set for other IT functions in the organisation; where the Internet had been driven by research, for example, the home page had also been at least partly driven and developed through research, although in most cases marketing departments were also involved. Very often external consultants were employed to develop the home page. In some cases the responsibility for development had evolved over time.

> *'The initial Web site was initiated by the IT department but we made sure that the marketing department had input. Now the marketing department is taking more responsibility.' IT Manager (GP)*

The two main reasons for developing the home page were marketing the organisation and the 'me too' syndrome.

> *'Competitive advantage initially, but as soon as you've thought about it and it's going to give me an edge, you suddenly realise that if I don't do it somebody else will, and.......then it's the 'me too' side'.' Senior Partner (GP)*
>
> *'It's two reasons, really. One is general marketing of the organisation…and secondly it's a bit of me too. We feel we should be there before anyone else does.' IT Manager (GP)*
>
> *'We felt we ought to be there because that's where everyone else was going then.' IT Manager (QS)*
>
> *'The feeling from the partnership generally was that our competitors have a Web site therefore we must have a Web site.' Head of Research (GP)*

Despite this there was a feeling that new clients would not be attracted exclusively from the Web. The personal nature of the property business was still a vital issue.

> *'It's not a primary marketing tool for the organisation. All the business is done on a one to one basis and traditional clients are not going to come as a result of the Web.' IT Manager (QS)*

Sometimes, however, Web pages were not updated regularly, which in the view of interviewees created problems.

> *'It's a very conservative firm and the Web site is very conservative. It hasn't changed since it started.' IT Manager (QS)*
>
> *'The site hasn't been changed or altered very much since it was set up.' Head of Research (GP)*

There was a view that as far as marketing property on the Internet was concerned, this was more likely to succeed for residential than commercial, but even so would generally only be part of the process leading to a successful conclusion to a deal.

> *'I think there's a lot of access to the Internet which may eventually be part of the process of leading to a deal. It certainly is not the only factor and you wouldn't see a property on the Internet and buy it, but indirectly the Internet does help.' IT Manager (GP)*

One interviewee felt that auctions of both commercial and residential property could be operated successfully using the Internet. Moreover, using the Internet to market property meant you didn't know your clients.

> 'The Web can help in the marketing of auctions both in commercial and residential quite a lot, we think. It's mass market. It's a short time-scale. The last thing we want to do is to put on a whole lot of investments or property investments where there's no relevance to a wide audience. There is a school of thought, quite well-established, that if you have to advertise a deal then you haven't done your job and you don't know your market. The downside of putting stuff on the Internet is that if you have to use the Internet it's too late.......A buyer will not generally respond to something he finds on the Internet because he knows a score of other people will have it as well.' Senior Partner (GP)

Nonetheless, there was considerable scepticism about whether the Internet would ever be used extensively for deals. For complex and expensive property investment deals and residential sales, personal contact and seeing the product could not be replaced easily, for example.

> 'People are quite happy buying CDs on the Internet but buying an investment property is a lot more complex. The Internet will probably help the professional surveyors to do their job, it will help to market properties, it will help to build up contacts. Ultimately the professional surveyors will still be required to do the deals... I think we're a very long way off from deals being done over the Internet.' IT Manager (GP)

> 'There's a lot of very impressive sites going up, but it's no more than billboarding. If a site generates an email contact then it's done its job. A lot of people are talking about ecommerce, but I cannot imagine anyone who's going to buy a quarter of a million pound house without ever going to see it, or talk to the agent and vendor...' Senior Partner (GP)

One interviewee pointed out that secrecy and confidentiality surrounding transaction data was a potential barrier to greater use of the Internet.

> 'If there was far more openness and every deal appeared on the Internet then people would use it to far greater effect.' IT Manager (GP)

Some GP firms did not use the home page for marketing property at all. In one case resistance had been encountered from the agency department, who felt they would lose control over potential buyers.

> 'There was a strong feeling from the agency department that they wanted to know where details were sent. We had debates over marketing property ...and asking users to register before going into the system. ' Head of Research (GP)

4.4.3 Using the Internet and the Impact on Professional Work

As far as GP surveying was concerned, EGi and Focus were used extensively.

> *'EGi is used a tremendous amount and Focus is also used. Some professional staff use it [the Internet] more than others..... I've heard a lot of praise for the Internet...There's very little criticism other than that you can't find what you want.' IT Manager (GP)*

Email had made a substantial impact in all the organisations concerned. As one interviewee put it:

> *'Nearly all drawings are coming on email and dedicated systems.' IT Manager (QS)*

There was a strong feeling that the 'information broker' role of the surveyor would not be threatened in the short term, but that inevitably, as time went on the role of surveyor would evolve towards an interpreter of information. In particular, 'disintermediation' could result in the residential agency market where Internet sales may increase.

> *'I think in residential you could possibly see that ['disintermediation'] happening. I think in commercial I would need a lot of convincing to agree with that..' Senior Partner (GP)*
>
> *'Any profession has its own barriers to entry to make its own job more valuable....The expertise that a surveyor ostensibly has... is that you know where to go and get the data. Now I accept that if you put it all on the Web then that data is open to all and then of course, de facto that removes the surveyor's job. Because there is an awful lot of information available and the speed of transacting a lot of business is increasing I still think there's going to be room for professionals who know how to handle the data quickly and...interpret it correctly. It's the same with solicitors..' Senior Partner (GP)*
>
> *'I think it's going to be more difficult for surveyors as time goes on because the assumption is they are going to have better knowledge and they're going to be required to know about deal X, Y and Z, and if it's all on the Internet then there's absolutely no defence for not knowing.' Senior Partner (GP)*
>
> *'More information on the net [means] the role of the surveyor is diminished. The view from the partners is...it is a threat to the business. My view is that gone are the days when you can charge people for what is essentially basic market data. The way you will make your money is that the client will get hold of the information on the Web, and say what do you think about this?' Head of Research (GP)*

One interviewee suggested that although the surveyor's role would change, the imperfect nature of the property market would prevent a serious erosion. Another danger was that information overload could result from more openness.

> *'It's bound to, but it's difficult to know exactly how much. We operate in a market place which....relies on imperfections of knowledge, disagreements over value, perceptions of value. If one had a perfect marketplace (defined by perfect knowledge) our job would be very, very, limited. I think the fact of it is we don't have a perfect market place ... there is an enormous diversity.... One of the challenges will be.... information overload.' Senior Partner (GP)*

In short, the ability to synthesise information would be important for both GP and QS surveyors.

> *'I do see the ability to assimilate relevant information and process it and present it in an intelligible way .....will be an increasingly important element.' Senior Partner (GP)*

Finally, it was felt that because of the generally 'flat' nature of surveying practices the Internet had not really impacted on organisational structure.

> *'Probably all chartered surveying practices have flat structures and it tends to be teams of people working on individual projects: a partner layer, a staff layer and an associate layer.... It's a fairly flat structure to begin with and whilst email has improved communication I don't think it's flattened our structure.' IT Manager (GP)*

4.4.4 Critical Success Factors

Although having an overall goal or aim is essential, developing too detailed a strategy for the Internet may be a hindrance. As one interviewee pointed out,

> *'I think that's one of the reasons why it's been successful: we didn't try too hard to formulate a strategy.' IT Manager (GP)*

It seems that the size of organisation is important here, however, as the relative cost to a small practice is higher if the path to Internet access is not as smooth as it was planned to be. There was, however, a view that, irrespective of size, organisations should grasp the Internet nettle rather than just talking about it, and this was based on shared experience.

> *'I think the main thing with the Internet and the Intranet is 'don't hold back'. Don't talk about it, do it, because it's one of those things that's a little bit intangible, quite difficult to come up with good business cases, but is actually quite a low cost investment. We've found that by doing something you can refine it and make it better. We started off with a simple Web and developed it.' IT Manager (GP).*
>
> *'If you have a larger agency side, marketing property is more important. We were more concerned about getting across the message that we had professional expertise in particular areas. If you're sitting there and you've got a computer and you're not connected to the outside world then information is a big thing. There's so much out there; there's so much for free. You've really got to start with that because it's easy: you need a modem, £14 per month for your subscription, and maybe also EGi. Rather than sitting around talking about it you should go ahead and get yourself out there...and look at other sites.' Head of Research (GP).*

One interviewee had encountered senior partner resistance but felt that the systems installed were a success.

> *'Persuading the senior partners that they needed it. There was a hell of a lot of resistance....they had lasted 150 years without it, why did they need it now? The success is that it's used so much.' IT Manager (QS)*

Involving the business as a whole in the development of the Internet was also very important.

> *'You must involve the business in designing the Internet and Intranet presence and so it mustn't be totally IT driven.' IT Manager (GP)*

There were important issues to consider, and security was raised by a number of interviewees, although it was important to get into perspective.

> *'You need not be overly worried about trusting people, security and things like that. Don't get hung up on issues that are important but are not the big hyped up problems the media say they are.' IT Manager (GP)*

The policies of organisations towards Internet access by staff also varied. It was recognised that the Internet could be used to view unsuitable material, but the policies towards access differed.

> *'It still happens that people use it for nefarious purpose.' Senior Partner (GP)*
>
> *'No restrictions. We leave it up to the conscience and behaviour of our individual people, and if they transgress then it's a serious offence.' Senior Partner (GP)*
>
> *'It's one of these things that I don't know the right answer. But I think that both extremes are actually dangerous. I think that the open approach that we've taken is very good because it doesn't restrict people's access to information, but you may not be able to stop people abusing that right. People will download software from the Internet and install that software on their PCs which cause support issues. ...People do use it to access non-business related information….and time is wasted in browsing for personal use.' IT Manager (GP)*
>
> *'There is a vast amount of useful material on the Internet and… we considered that we could and should be able to trust our professional staff to access the Internet generally and be responsible in their use. ' IT Manager (GP)*

As regards training and education, some organisations had no formal training on the use of the Internet or other IT skills and others used 'cascade' training, where one person is trained and acts as coach or trainer to others. One large practice has introduced 'cyber breakfasts', which are run in-house to train professional staff on the use of the Internet.

4.4.5 *Future Developments*

A number of organisations are introducing Intranets, which is seen as a very effective way of promoting internal communication.

> *'We're looking to go down an Intranet route for internal documents. It has proved to be an expensive and time-consuming solution, but it's something we're going to have to try to do. Our Intranet will give access to the Web.' Senior Partner (GP)*
>
> *'The advantage of an Intranet is shared data. Things like a library of photographs that people can pull down.' IT Manager (QS)*
>
> *'The Intranet has been used for mainly improving Internal communication around the firm and for the information centre for making databases available. A lot of the sharing of information on the Intranet is carrying out functions that Lotus Notes would be used for.' IT Manager (GP)*

Another organisation was considering the development of an Extranet.

> '*We're more looking at the Extranet and how to bring clients in, and that's why we're using Lotus Notes to bringing security. The net provides an easy pipe to get in with and we may well give or encourage clients to buy Notes. If you can target your top 100 or 200 clients....You want to give them more information than you might perhaps put up on a site that was largely just advertising.' IT Manager (GP)*

As far as changing property requirements were concerned, it was generally felt that the Internet and related technology would not impact on markets and space requirements in the short term, although in the long term there is likely to be an effect. One interviewee felt this would be most marked in the City of London. Another organisation is actively looking at how to alter the balance of space requirements in its own offices through teleworking and other innovations.

Finally, it was felt that finding information on the Web was often time-consuming, and that there was a need for an all-embracing property information search engine.

> '*What is needed is a universal search engine for all this data. The information is currently too fragmented.' Head of Research (GP)*

5. SUMMARY AND CONCLUSIONS

5.1 Introduction

The overall aim of this study has been to provide a detailed snapshot of Internet and Intranet use within the property profession, by selecting three main groups: GP and QS practices and corporates. In addition, the key objectives of the research were to answer the following questions:

- what is the level of Internet and Intranet usage and what are the attitudes of surveyors towards them?

- what are the 'critical success factors' (or 'drivers') which operate in enabling professional surveying practices of varying size to introduce and use the Internet in the best way?

- what are the 'barriers' to the successful introduction of the Internet and how can they be overcome?

- what are the key benefits for organisations using the Internet?

- how will the Internet affect professional work and the property requirements of clients?

This final chapter briefly summarises the main results before setting out the main conclusions and implications for the property profession.

5.2 Summary

5.2.1 IT Profile of the Property Profession

- Despite the recent RICS Survey (Honey (1997)), previous research had shown the property profession still coming to terms with IT. The current survey, however, confirms the view that as far as IT is concerned, most organisations (some 97% of the sample), whatever their size, now have access to IT.

- A majority of respondents (53%) had a formal IT strategy but this was more common in larger organisations and corporates, rather than GP and QS.

- Most organisations were networked (65.6%) and again this was more common in larger organisations and corporates.

5.2.2 The Internet

Access
- Email access is commonplace in the property profession. Some 69% of respondents had access to email, and the primary use is 'communication

with customers/clients' (81.7% of all cases). Increased efficiency was the most important reason for its introduction.

- Access to the Web is provided in the majority (56.3%) of organisations, with 'research' (74.3% of cases) as the most important use overall.

- An Internet access policy was present in only 35% of organisations, and was most common in corporates. Nefarious use of the Internet was a major concern.

- Some 34% of all organisations in the survey had a home page, and the figure was highest amongst corporates, 46.2%, compared with 33.6% GP and 26.6% QS. The period since 1995 had seen the most rapid growth in Web sites.

5.2.3 Intranets

- Only 16.9% of organisations had Intranets, and with Intranets the primary uses are 'company information' (80.9% of cases), and 'email' (66% of cases). Some 44% of corporates had Intranets.

- Nationally networked offices in the UK dominated in 60.5% of cases.

- The pattern of Intranet growth mirrors that of the Internet in the respondent sample with major growth occurring since 1995.

- The main driving force for the Internet has come from the IT department (in 68.3% of organisations with Intranets).

One of the case studies showed that an Extranet can be used to bring clients closer to the company or practice, and to share data and information.

5.2.4 Evolution and Use of the Internet

The case studies showed that Internet access had often evolved in organisations from a pre-existing computer network. In many cases (40% in the postal survey) the driving force for the Internet had come from the IT department, but in small organisations, the sole practitioner or principal was the key driving force.

Two key reasons for developing a home page were marketing the organisation and the 'me too' syndrome, but it was important for practices to realise that, in particular, new clients would not be attracted exclusively from the Web. The personal nature of property was still vital to consider.

The case studies indicated that as far as marketing property on the Internet was concerned, this was more likely to succeed in residential than commercial, but even so was only part of the process of concluding a deal.

Moreover, there was considerable scepticism over whether the Internet would ever be used extensively for deals because of:

- the nature of the product;

- the complexity of the transaction process;

- the need for face-to-face contact;

- the continuing secrecy/confidentiality over deals/transactions data.

This was borne out by the fact that the Web was used for property 'marketing/comparables' in 33.3% of cases compared with 71.8% for 'research', although the former use was more frequent in the GP/corporate groups.

5.2.5 *The Impact on Professional Work*

Email had made a substantial impact in all organisations. The most important reason for introducing email was 'to increase efficiency', and the case studies revealed that in the case of one QS firm (Case Study 6 in Appendix 4) nearly all drawings were sent on email and dedicated systems.

The postal survey revealed that surveyors:

- **do not** feel their role as 'information broker' is under threat;

- **do not** think the Internet will impact on the location and occupancy of businesses in the short term.

Surveyors **do** feel, however, that they should understand and use the Internet to maintain their competitive advantage.

The issue of 'disintermediation' was explored in more detail in the Case Studies. The view from the postal questionnaire was confirmed to a large degree: namely, that the information brokerage role of the GP and QS surveyor would not be threatened in the short-term, but over the next 5-10 years the role of the surveyor would, inevitably, shift towards an 'interpreter' and 'manager' of more readily available information, rather as Doherty (op. cit.) and others cited in Chapter 2 of this report suggest. In particular, 'disintermediation' could result in the residential agency market where Internet sales could increase. This should be tempered by the comments made above in relation to marketing property on the Internet, however. Moreover, property market imperfections would continue to prevent a serious erosion of the surveyor's role.

Finally, it was felt that the Internet had not changed surveying practices' structures, because they tended to operate with fairly 'flat' structures anyway.

5.2.6 *'Critical Success Factors' or 'Drivers'*

The four most important 'critical success factors' (CSFs), or 'drivers', which promote Internet and Intranet use are:

- 'senior management support'

- 'existing IT culture';

- 'involvement of all staff'; and

- 'formal IT strategy'.

It clearly is important to have support from the practice partnership or the board of directors in a company. The positive culture of IT in an organisation can also promote use. If organisations view IT as an important and vital tool they are more likely to use the Internet. Involving all staff in the implementation of the Internet means employees 'buy in' more readily to the new technology. Finally, a formal IT strategy, to which the Internet is linked, is important to have in place.

However, the size and type of organisation also plays a part: statistical testing revealed that larger organisations rated 'existing IT culture' and 'formal IT strategy' more highly than smaller ones, and that corporates felt the presence of a 'formal IT strategy' was more important than GP and QS.

The case studies confirmed these views and highlighted key issues:

- ***Involving the Business.*** Involving the business as a whole in the development of the Internet, and not just the IT department, was very important. Often marketing departments became involved in home page development and it was also important to update the page regularly and review its development.

- ***Get onto the Internet.*** Although an overall plan or goal for Internet development and linking it to the IT strategy was fundamental, getting onto the Internet rather than 'just talking about it' was important, whatever the size of organisation.

- ***Persuade Others.*** There was much resistance to the Internet, particularly by more senior members of staff who saw it as a threat. 'Champions for change' were needed in such cases to persuade and argue the case for the new technology.

- ***Training and Education.*** This was a vital component for users of the Internet, as evidenced by the use of 'cyber breakfasts' in one organisation. Indeed, although 'training and education' only has a mean rating of 2.28 compared with 'formal IT strategy' of 2.39 in the main survey, the difference is small.

5.2.7 Barriers to Internet Use

The four most important barriers to Internet use were:

- 'speed';
- 'lack of security';
- 'legal/confidentiality issues'; and
- 'costs'.

However, 'time-consuming' and 'time-wasting' were also important as a major part of the 'other' category.

These issues have often been raised in previous surveys (DTI (op. cit.)). The slow speed of Internet access poses particular problems where there is no dedicated link. Security issues, particularly in relation to the transmission of clients' details, were highlighted as a particular fear, and allied with this is the potential nefarious use by employees. Firewalls and Internet access policies can overcome such problems, however.

The costs of Internet access, 'legal/confidentiality issues' and 'threat to professional work' were considered to be more important by those without Internet access than those with access and this was found to be statistically significant. This suggests preconceptions need to be changed to overcome the barriers and promote the benefits of use.

There were also size and type of organisation differences: large organisations were more concerned about security than smaller ones, and corporates rated 'lack of security' and 'legal/confidentiality' issues higher than QS and GP, which was a statistically significant result.

5.2.8 Benefits of Internet Use

The three most important benefits of Internet use were found to be:

- 'increased competitive advantage';
- 'reduced communication costs'; and
- 'reduced cost of sharing information'.

'Increased productivity' was also important. Maintaining a competitive edge had clearly been a major reason for developing company Web sites, as was shown by the case studies. Moreover email was a vital tool which reduced communication costs. Finally, email and the Web enable employees and clients to share information more easily than before.

None of the differences by size and type of organisation between the various benefits was found to be statistically significant (see Section 4.3.8).

5.2.9 The Importance of Size and Type of Organisation

The previous research outlined in Chapter 2 showed how SMEs had often failed to embrace the new technology. The results from the current research show that although small GP and QS practices do have access to IT they have still some way to go to embrace the Internet and Intranet to the same extent as larger practices.

For example, the current research found that statistically,

- the greater the size of organisation (of whatever type) the more likely it is to have email, Web and Intranet access, and

- corporates are more likely to have Intranet access than GP and QS.

For example, figure 5-1 shows the size differences between GP and QS very clearly, in terms of access to PCs, email, Internet, Intranets and presence of a home page. Fewer, smaller organisations had Web access, for example, than larger ones: eg 20.9% of small GP compared with 55.6% very large GP.

Figure 5-1 Size Comparison of GP and QS Groups

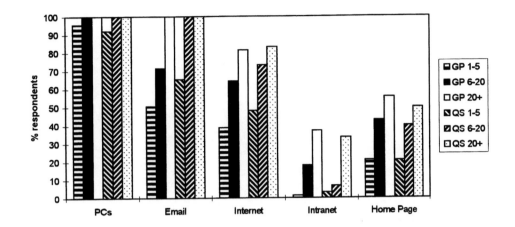

In many cases, corporates have the benefits of a well-developed IT culture so that the 'property department' of a large company has also 'bought into' the IT strategy and support. Professional practices often, however, lack these advantages, again because many of them are sole practitioners, and so factors such as the costs of Internet access can seem insurmountable to a company on a limited budget. Figure 5.2 shows, for example, how corporates have higher levels of PC, email, Internet, Intranet and home page access than GP and QS.

Figure 5-2 Organisation Type Comparisons

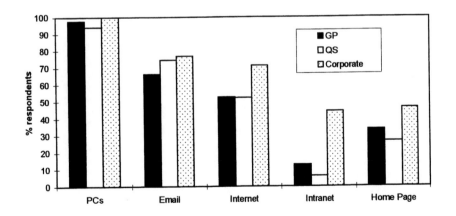

5.3 Conclusions and Implications

5.3.1 Previous Research and Scope of Current Research

As Table 5-1 shows, the sample in the current research compares favourably with the DTI (1998) survey in terms of its levels of access to the Internet and Intranet.

Table 5-1 Comparison of DTI (1998) and Current Research

	DTI	Current Research[1]
Email Used	63%	68.9%
Internet Access	49%	56.3%
Intranet Access	14%	16.9%
Home Page	27%	33%

Note [1] Base=All respondents

However, the current research presents unweighted results, which we know do not reflect the fact that, in the real world, the GP and QS groups contain large numbers of very small practices not having as extensive PC and Internet access as the medium/large and very large size groups. The nature of the sampling technique used in this research means that, proportionately, these small practices are under-represented in the final sample (see sections 3.2 and 4.2 and Tables A1 and A2 of Appendix 2). The survey results, however, can be relied upon as a good guide to the level of access for this particular sample, although the levels of access for the profession as a whole are likely to be less because of the preponderance of very small practices.

5.3.2 Policy Implications

Comments from respondents' questionnaires and the case studies suggested there are two main initiatives that the RICS could develop:

- Further IT guidance and support for prospective Internet users. The RICS has a number of IT panels (for example, the 'Information Management Panel' and 'Construction IT') and has developed an Information Markets Strategy (further information is at www.rics.org.uk). However, the property profession still lacks an overarching IT business support function. The Institute of Chartered Accountants in England and Wales, for example, has an 'IT Faculty' (www.icaew.co.uk/depts/td/tditf/welcome.htm), which through its newsletter, booklets, bulletin boards and seminars, presents technical information for members at a low subscription; and,

- More information on how the Internet can help small practices, with perhaps a Web site providing relevant information and links to the DTI Information Society Initiative and Internet information.

In addition there should be a better way of accessing property information on the Web through a specialist search engine. Some sites such as the Property Information Mall and Focusnet go some way towards this but there is a lot of relevant property information that continues to be overlooked.

5.3.3 A Model of Drivers and Barriers

The research also enables us to build a simple model of the drivers and barriers to Internet/Intranet access for the property profession, as figure 5.2

shows. These should be viewed in the context of what might be called 'intrinsic' factors (Dixon (1994)), such as size and type of organisation and whether an organisation already has Internet access. These were found to be statistically associated with a number of the drivers and barriers (see sections 4.3.8 and 5.2.9). For example, the larger the organisation the more likely it is to have email, Web and Intranet access.

Figure 5-3 A Simple Model of Drivers and Barriers

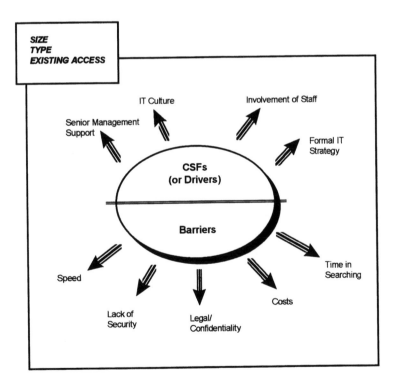

respondents recognised, understanding and using the Internet is a key to the profession's development.

As one respondent, from a small practice, put it:

> *'Information is the key to make good business decisions and increasing market share. We plan to go onto the Internet in 1998 because we know we have to in order to remain competitive.'*

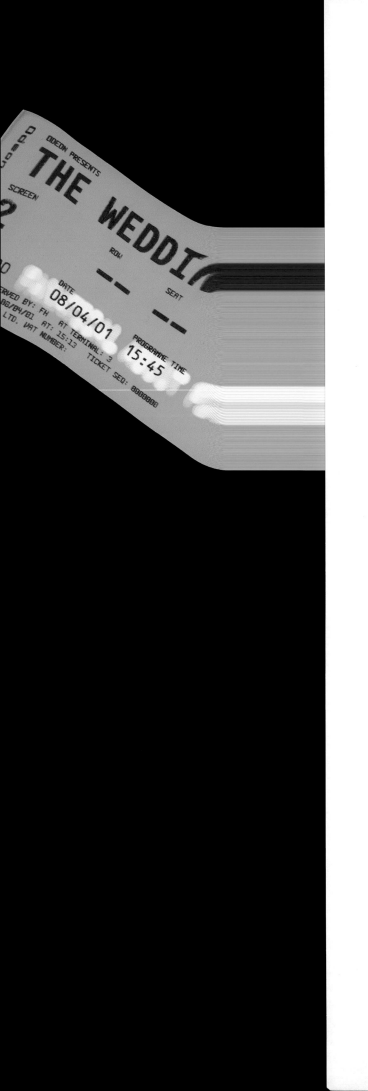

6. BIBLIOGRAPHY

Aspect Control Consulting (1996) <u>Access Control Timebomb</u>, ACC.

Bowen,D. (1997) <u>The Net Profit Guide to Business on the Internet</u>, Net Profit Publications.

Bridges,A. (1996) <u>The Construction Net: Online Information Services for the Construction Industry</u>, E. & F.N. Spon.

Brummer, A. (1998) 'Dash for Cash in the Online Market Place', <u>The Guardian</u>, May 27.

Cairncross,F. (1997) <u>The Death of Distance</u>, Orion Business Books.

Cameron,D. (1995) <u>Implementing the Internet for Business</u>, Computer Technology Group.

Construction Industry Computing Association (CICA) (1995) <u>Building IT 2005</u>, CICA.

CMG (1997) <u>Intranet Survey</u>, CMG.

Cyberkix (1997) <u>How Small and Medium Enterprises are Implementing the Internet</u>, Cyberkix.

Davis,L. (1997) 'Wired up to a brave new world', <u>CSM</u>, Jan. 34-35.

DFEE (1997) <u>Connecting the Learning Society</u>, Department for Further Education.

Dixon, T.J. (1994) <u>IT Skills Training and Education for the Surveying Profession: Requirements for the 1990s</u>, College of Estate Management.

Doherty,P. (1997<u>) Cyberplaces: The Internet Guide for Architects, Engineers and Contractors</u>, R.S. Means.

DTI (1996) <u>Development of the Information Society: An International Analysis</u>, DTI.

DTI (1997<u>) Moving into the Information Society: An International Benchmarking Study</u>, DTI.

DTI (1998) <u>Moving into the Information Age: International Benchmarking Study</u>, DTI.

Earl,M.J. (1989) <u>Management Strategies for Information Technology</u>, Prentice Hall.

Edkins,S. (1997) 'The Internet's Use in the Construction Industry' <u>Unpublished MBA Thesis</u>, Department of Construction Management, Reading University.

Evans, P., and Wurster, T. (1997) 'Strategy and the New Economics of Information', <u>Harvard Business Review</u>, 71-82, Sept-Oct.

Finch,E. (1996) <u>The Internet for Property Professionals</u>, CEM.

Garvey,A. (1997) 'The Intranet: A unique opportunity if...', <u>IT Training</u>, June 59-62.

Ginarlis, J. (1997) <u>Pensions Revolution</u>, CSC Financial Services.

Glueck,W.F. (1980) Business Policy and Strategic Management, McGraw Hill.

Haddock,M. (1996) 'The Internet and the Property Professional, Property Review, April, 77-79.

Hargitay,S., & Dixon,T.J. (1989) Software Selection for Surveyors, Macmillan.

Honey,R. (1997) 'Assessing the Impact of the Internet on Past and Future Property Markets', Conference Paper EGi: Maximising the Opportunities of the Internet in the Property Market, September.

Howard,R. (1998) Computing in Construction: Pioneers and the Future, Butterworth/Heinneman.

Judge,P. & Ogg,C. (1997) 'The Intranet Report: Web Technology for Enterprise Information Management, Elan.

Kearney,A.T. (Management Consultants) (1994) The Barriers and Opportunities of Information Technology - A Management Perspective, AT Kearney, London.

Kennedy,P. (1998) The Internet and the World Wide Web: Rough Guide, Penguin.

KPMG (1996) The Internet : A Guide for Business Users, KPMG.

Lawson,D. (1997a) 'Terminal Velocity', Property Week, 17 October, 33-35.

Lawson, D. (1997b) 'Net Receipts', Property Week, 12 Sept., 37-8.

Markham,J. (1998) The Future of Shopping: Traditional Patterns and Net Effects, Macmillan.

McBride,N. (1997) 'Business Use of the Internet: Strategic Revision or Just another bandwagon', European Management Journal, February, 58-67.

Porter,M. (1980) Competitive Strategy, Free Press.

REATEA (1997) Technology in Residential Estate Agency, REATEA.

RICS (1997a) World Wide Web Sites for Chartered Surveyors, RICS.

RICS (1997b) RICS 1997 Survey of Members, RICS/BPRI.

RICS (1997c) Surveying the Superhighway: A Guide to the Internet for Chartered Surveyors, RICS.

RICS (1997d) Directory Of Members, RICS.

Rowley, S., Fisher, P, and Holmes, A. (1998) 'A National Valuation Evidence Database: The Future of Valuation Data Provision', Journal of Property Valuation and Investment, Vol 16 No 1, 99-108.

Society of Property Researchers (SPR) (1995) The Adequacy and Accuracy of Commercial Property Data, SPR.

Sullivan,K. (1993) The Strategic Use of IT (RICS Survey), South Bank University/RICS (unpublished).

Szuptowicz,B.O. (1997) Intranets and Groupware: Effective Communications for the Enterprise.

Tapscott,D. (1996) The Digital Economy: Promise and Peril in the Age of Networked Intelligence, McGraw Hill.

Temple, P (1997) <u>The Online Investor: Levelling the Information Playing Field</u>, John Wiley.

Tinworth, A. (1997) 'Anywhere, Any place, Any time', <u>Estates Gazette</u>, Oct 18, 157-9.

University of Reading (1997) <u>Right Space Right Time</u>, Dept of Land Management, (RICS).

US Chamber of Commerce (1998) <u>The Emerging Digital Economy</u>, US Chamber of Commerce.

Weintraut, J.N. (1997) 'Introduction' in Reid,R.H. <u>Architects of the Web</u>, Wiley.

Weiss, E. (1997) 'US Commercial and Residential Property Marketing on the Internet', <u>Conference Paper EGi: Maximising the Opportunities of the Internet in the Property Market</u>, September.

Widdifield, R., and Grover,V. (1995) 'Internet and the Implications of the Information Superhighway for Business', <u>Journal of System Management</u>, May-June, 16-65.

Wyatt,P. (1996) 'How Property Can Benefit from the Superhighway', <u>CSM</u>, October, 21.

APPENDICES

APPENDIX 1: QUESTIONNAIRE

**THE COLLEGE
OF ESTATE
MANAGEMENT**

Questionnaire:
The Impact of the Internet on the Surveying Profession

As you may know, the RICS has recently introduced a number of IT initiatives and the College of Estate Management is seeking to build on this by producing a clearer picture of how the Internet (and related technology such as email and intranets) is being used today by the surveying profession, and how it will impact in the future.

This questionnaire is being sent to a large sample of surveying professionals, as part of a major research project and report funded by the RICS Education Trust and the Pat Allsop Trust. We hope as a result of this to obtain a better idea of how you and other professionals are using the Internet, and how you view its advantages and disadvantages. Even if your organisation does not use the Internet we would still like to hear your views.

Some of the questions may need to be answered by your IT manager, but the questionnaire should take you only about 15 minutes to complete.

We do hope you will be able to respond and please would you return the questionnaire in the pre-paid envelope by *31 March at the latest to*:

Dr Tim Dixon
Director of Research
College of Estate Management
Whiteknights
Reading RG6 6AW

If you respond we will send you a copy of the executive summary of results when it is completed.

Your help is much appreciated and all information you provide will be treated in a confidential manner. If you would like any further information please contact Tim Dixon on 0118 9861101 (email: t.j.dixon@reading.ac.uk).

1.0 You and Your Organisation

1.1 What is the name of your organisation?

_____

1.2 What is your name?

_____

1.3 What is your title/position?

_____

1.4 How many partners does your organisation have at your location?
- O 1 - 5
- O 6 - 10
- O 11 - 20
- O 21 - 50
- O More than 50

1.5 Approximately how many employees does your company have at your location?
- O 1-9
- O 10-20
- O 21-30
- O 31-50
- O more than 50

1.6 What is the geographic distribution of your company?
- O One site only in the UK
- O More than one site locally
- O More than one site regionally
- O More than one site nationally
- O More than one site internationally

1.7 To which of the following RICS market areas is the work of your organisation most closely related?
- ❑ Commercial Property
- ❑ Construction
- ❑ Residential Property
- ❑ Other _____

1.8 Does your organisation have a separate IT department or IT support staff?
- O Yes
- O No

2.0 PCs and Networking

2.1 Does your organisation have a formal IT strategy?
- O Yes
- O No

2.2 Which of the following are used by employees in your organisation?
- ❑ Computers/PC/Workstations
- ❑ Computers/PCs with CD-ROMs
- ❑ Computers/PCs with modems
- ❑ Laptops/Notebooks/Mobile Computers
- ❑ None

If you ticked 'None' go to Question 2.3; otherwise Question 2.4

2.3 Why does your company not use PCs? (please rank in order of importance: 1= most important and 4 least important)

	Rank
O No need for IT	_____
O IT is too expensive	_____
O Need to know more about IT	_____
O Other _____	_____

Please go to Question 4.2 on the last page of this questionnaire

2.4 Are computers and PCs networked in the organisation?
- O Yes - *go to Question 3.1*
- O No - *go to Question 2.5*

2.5 If NO to question 2.4, for which of the following reasons is your organisation not networked?
- ❑ Only one computer/PC
- ❑ Currently in process of networking
- ❑ No need for networking
- ❑ Networking is too expensive
- ❑ Networks are unreliable
- ❑ Need to improve understanding
- ❑ Other _____

1

3.0 The Internet and Intranets

In this section of the questionnaire we ask you some questions about the internet and intranets. For the purposes of this research 'Internet' is defined as the worldwide network of computers comprising email and the World Wide Web. An 'Intranet' is defined as an internal private secure network running the internet protocol.

3.1 To what extent does your organisation use internal/external email? (please tick one only)

- O Not used and no plans to use
- O Not used but plans within next 6 months
- O Not used but considering it for the long term
- O Rarely
- O Occasionally
- O Quite Often
- O Frequently

3.2 For which of the following reasons is internet email used?

- ❑ Communication within a site
- ❑ Communication between local sites
- ❑ Communication between national sites
- ❑ Communication between international sites
- ❑ Communication with customers/clients
- ❑ Communication with others
- ❑ Other (please specify) _____

3.3 Why was email first introduced in your organisation? (Please rank in order of importance: 1 = most important and 4 = least important)

	Rank
O To increase efficiency	_____
O Customers'/clients' requests	_____
O To maintain competitive edge	_____
O Other (please specify) _____	_____

3.4 Do employees in your organisation have access to the internet other than for email use (ie to the World Wide Web)? (Please tick one only)

- O No access and no plans for access
- O No current access but within next 6 months
- O Yes - access from shared PCs
- O Other (please specify) _____

3.5 What do employees in your organisation use the internet and World Wide Web for?
- ❑ Advertising/Marketing
- ❑ Marketing Comparables
- ❑ Research
- ❑ Business Contacts
- ❑ Information on Competitors
- ❑ News
- ❑ Market Trends
- ❑ Other (please specify) _____

3.6 Does your organisation have a formal internet access policy for employees?

- O Yes
- O No

3.7 Which department in your organisation has been the driving force for the development of the internet and website?

- ❑ IT
- ❑ Marketing
- ❑ Other (please specify)—————————

3.8 Does your company have a site on the World Wide Web (ie a home page)?

- O Yes
- O No

3.9 What is the name of your internet service provider?

_____

3.10 What is the main home page address?

www. _____

3.11 Approximately how many 'hits' (or visits) per month does the web site have?

_____

3.12 When was the home page set up?

_____

3.13 How important are the following barriers to your organisation's use of the internet?

Please circle the relevant numbers	Not important			Very important
Lack of security	1	2	3	4
Speed	1	2	3	4
Threat to professional work	1	2	3	4
Congestion	1	2	3	4
Costs	1	2	3	4
Too much information	1	2	3	4
Legal/confidentiality issues	1	2	3	4
Other _____	1	2	3	4

2

3.14 What are the benefits of your organisation's use of the internet?

Please circle the relevant numbers	Not important			Very important
Increased revenue	1	2	3	4
Increased productivity	1	2	3	4
Reduced communication costs	1	2	3	4
Reduced cost of sharing information	1	2	3	4
Increased competitive advantage	1	2	3	4
Other _____	1	2	3	4

3.15 Has your organisation set up an intranet?

- O Yes - go to question 3.16
- O No and no plans to do so - go to question 4.1
- O No but plan within 6 mths - go to question 4.1

3.16 For what services does your company use the intranet?

- ❏ Document Transfer
- ❏ Company information
- ❏ Email
- ❏ Access to websites
- ❏ Other (please specify) _____

3.17 Does your intranet link different offices?

- ❏ No
- ❏ Yes - in the UK
- ❏ Yes - internationally

3.18 When was the intranet set up? _____

3.19 Which department in your organisation has been the driving force for the development of the intranet?

- ❏ IT
- ❏ Marketing
- ❏ Other (please specify) _____

4.0 Additional Questions

4.1 Which of the following have been important in promoting the use of the internet/intranet in your organisation?

Please circle the relevant numbers	Not important			Very important
Existing IT culture	1	2	3	4
Senior management support	1	2	3	4
Involvement of all staff	1	2	3	4
Formal IT strategy	1	2	3	4
Linkage to business plan	1	2	3	4
Training and education plan	1	2	3	4
Other_____	1	2	3	4

4.2 What is your reaction to the following statements?

Please circle the relevant numbers	Disagree Strongly			Agree Strongly
The internet will replace the surveyor's role as information broker	1	2	3	4
The internet will soon impact on the location/and occupancy of our clients' businesses	1	2	3	4
Surveyors must understand and use the internet to maintain their competitive advantage	1	2	3	4

4.3 What additional comments would you like to make about the internet and intranet and its impact on the surveying profession?

_____

_____

_____

4.4 Would you be willing for your organisation to be used as a case study example for this research? This would involve a further interview.

- O Yes
- O No

Signature _____

Date _____

Thank you very much for taking the time and trouble to complete this questionnaire. If you have any queries please contact Dr Tim Dixon at The College of Estate Management. You will receive a copy of the results in the form of an executive summary in due course.

3

APPENDIX 2: TABLES OF RESULTS

Notes to the Tables

In the tables which follow, the base for each table is the number of respondents to the questionnaire unless otherwise stated.

The tables present unweighted results, as explained in section 4.2 of the report.

Some tables are based on 'multiple response' questions, in which case the 'responses' column exceeds the number of respondents, and the 'cases %' column is more than 100%. This is because respondents answer 'Yes' to more than one option in these questions.

The 'Size' category in the relevant tables refers to the number of partners/directors in an organisation.

Non-Response and Weighted Results Comparison

Table A1 Non-Respondents and Respondents (% answering yes)

	General Practice				Quantity Surveying			
	1-5 Non-Resp.	1-5 Resp.	6-20 Non-Resp.	6-20 Resp	1-5 Non-Resp.	1-5 Resp.	6-20 Non-Resp.	6-20 Resp.
Use of PCs	85%	95.7%	100%	100%	80%	92%	100%	100%
Use of Email	24%	48.5%	85%	71.5%	44%	64.7%	95%	60%
Use of Internet	29%	37.1%	85%	64.2%	31%	44.4%	85%	73.3%

Notes: This table compares the percentages of non-respondents and respondents answering yes to whether the organisation has PCs, uses email and uses the Internet.

Table A2 Unweighted and Weighted Results (% answering yes)

	Unweighted General Practice	Weighted General Practice	Unweighted Quantity Surveying	Weighted Quantity Surveying
Use of PCs	97.6%	52.2%	94.05%	66.57%
Use of Email	64.8%	26.7%	70.24%	43.8%
Use of Internet	52.8%	20.5%	52.38%	32.3%
With Home Page	32.8%	11.15%	25%	13.92%
With Intranet	12.8%	0.98%	5.95%	2.33%

Notes: This table compares the percentages of unweighted and weighted responses in the GP and QS subgroups. The weights applied are based on the proportions of practices in each size category from the population as a whole (based on Table 3.2 in the main report). Because of the low response rate in very large QS firms the weighted results should be treated with caution, and there are other valid reasons for presenting only unweighted results (see sections 3.2 and 4.2).

You and Your Organisation

Table B1 Respondents by Organisation Type

	Count	%
General Practice surveying	125	47.9%
Quantity surveying	84	32.2%
Corporate	52	19.9%
Total	261	100.0%

Table B2 Respondents by Job Title (Q1.3)

	Count	%
Principal/ Sole Principal	46	17.9%
Senior Partner/Partner	63	24.5%
IT Partner	3	1.2%
Director	48	18.7%
IT Manager	24	9.3%
Other	73	28.4%
Total	257	100.0%

Table B3 Respondents by Organisation Type and Job Title (Q1.3)

	General Practice Surveying		Quantity Surveying		Corporate	
	Count	%	Count	%	Count	%
Principal/Sole Principal	25	20.2%	21	25.3%		
Senior Partner/Partner	41	33.1%	22	26.5%		
IT Partner	1	.8%	2	2.4%		
Director	13	10.5%	17	20.5%	18	36.0%
IT Manager	15	12.1%	6	7.2%	3	6.0%
Other	29	23.4%	15	18.1%	29	58.0%
Total	124	100.0%	83	100.0%	50	100.0%

Table B4 Respondents by Organisation Type and Size (Q1.4)

	General Practice Surveying		Quantity surveying		Corporate	
	Count	%	Count	%	Count	%
Small	70	56.0%	63	75.0%	17	32.7%
Medium/Large	28	22.4%	15	17.9%	5	9.6%
Very Large	27	21.6%	6	7.1%	30	57.7%
Total	125	100.0%	84	100.0%	52	100.0%

Table B5 Respondents by Organisation Type and Number of Employees (Q1.5)

	General Practice Surveying		Quantity surveying		Corporate	
	Count	%	Count	%	Count	%
1-9	49	39.8%	34	42.5%	11	21.2%
10-20	21	17.1%	15	18.8%	6	11.5%
21-30	15	12.2%	8	10.0%	3	5.8%
31-50	8	6.5%	7	8.8%	8	15.4%
>50	30	24.4%	16	20.0%	24	46.2%
Total	123	100.0%	80	100.0%	52	100.0%

Table B6 Respondents by Organisation Type and Geographical Location (Q1.6)

	General Practice Surveying		Quantity surveying		Corporate	
	Count	%	Count	%	Count	%
One site only in the UK	43	35.0%	36	42.9%	16	31.4%
More than one site locally	22	17.9%	3	3.6%	3	5.9%
More than one site regionally	22	17.9%	10	11.9%	2	3.9%
More than one site nationally	24	19.5%	22	26.2%	19	37.3%
More than one site internationally	12	9.8%	13	15.5%	11	21.6%
Total	123	100.0%	84	100.0%	51	100.0%

Table B7 Respondents by RICS Market Areas (Q1.7)

	Responses	Cases %
Commercial property	143	57.4%
Construction	95	38.2%
Residential	74	29.7%
Total	312	125.3%

Table B8 Separate IT Department or Support (Q1.8)

	Count	%
Yes	98	37.5%
No	163	62.5%
Total	261	100.0%

Table B9 Separate IT Department or Support by Organisation Type (Q1.8)

	General Practice surveying	Quantity surveying	Corporate
Yes	30.4%	27.4%	71.2%
No	69.6%	72.6%	28.8%
Total	100.0%	100.0%	100.0%

Table B10 Separate IT Department or Support by Organisation Type and Size (Q1.8)

	General Practice surveying			Quantity surveying			Corporate		
	Small (1-5)	Medium/ Large (6-20)	Very Large (>20)	Small (1-5)	Medium /Large (6-20)	Very Large (>20)	Small (1-5)	Medium /Large (6-20)	Very Large (>20)
Yes	8.6%	35.7%	81.5%	15.9%	53.3%	83.3%	47.1%	40.0%	90.0%
No	91.4%	64.3%	18.5%	84.1%	46.7%	16.7%	52.9%	60.0%	10.0%
Total	100.0%	100.0%	100.0%	100.0%	100.0%	100.0%	100.0%	100.0%	100.0%

PCs and Networking

Table B11 Presence of IT Strategy (Q2.1)

	Count	%
Yes	138	53.3%
No	121	46.7%
Total	259	100.0%

Table B12 Presence of IT Strategy by Organisation Type (Q2.1)

	General Practice surveying	Quantity surveying	Corporate
Yes	45.2%	50.0%	78.4%
No	54.8%	50.0%	21.6%
Total	100.0%	100.0%	100.0%

Table B13 Presence of IT Strategy by Organisation Type and Size (Q2.1)

	General Practice surveying			Quantity surveying			Corporate		
	Small (1-5)	Medium/ Large (6-20)	Very Large (>20)	Small (1-5)	Medium/ Large (6-20)	Very Large (>20)	Small (1-5)	Medium/ Large (6-20)	Very Large (>20)
Yes	20.3%	60.7%	92.6%	34.9%	93.3%	100.0%	58.8%	80.0%	89.7%
No	79.7%	39.3%	7.4%	65.1%	6.7%		41.2%	20.0%	10.3%
Total	100.0%	100.0%	100.0%	100.0%	100.0%	100.0%	100.0%	100.0%	100.0%

Table B14 PCs Used (Q2.2)

	Count	%
No PCs	8	3.1%
PCs	253	96.9%
Total	261	100.0%

Table B15 PCs Used (Q2.2)

	General Practice surveying	Quantity surveying	Corporate
No PCs	2.4%	6.0%	
PCs	97.6%	94.0%	100.0%
Total	100.0%	100.0%	100.0%

Table B16 Type of PC Used (Q2.2)

	Responses	Cases %
Computers/PC/ Workstations	197	78.8%
Computers/PCs with CD-ROMs	197	78.8%
Computers/PCs with modems	189	75.6%
Laptops/Notebooks/ Mobiles	142	56.8%
Total	725	290.0%

Table B17 Type of PC Used by Organisation Type (Q2.2)

	General Practice surveying	Quantity surveying	Corporate
Computers/PC/ Workstations	77.5%	78.2%	82.7%
Computers/PCs with CD-ROMs	80.0%	80.8%	73.1%
Computers/PCs with modems	74.2%	78.2%	75.0%
Laptops/Notebooks/ Mobiles	48.3%	62.8%	67.3%
Total	280.0%	300.0%	298.1%

Table B18 Type of PC Used by Organisation Type and Size (Q2.2)

	General Practice surveying			Quantity surveying			Corporate		
	Small (1-5)	Medium/ Large (6-20)	Very Large (>20)	Small (1-5)	Medium/ Large (6-20)	Very Large (>20)	Small (1-5)	Medium/ Large (6-20)	Very Large (>20)
	Cases %	Cases %	Cases %	Cases %	Cases %	Cases %	Cases %	Cases %	Cases %
Computers/ PC/ Workstations	64.6%	89.3%	96.3%	75.9%	86.7%	80.0%	64.7%	100.0%	90.0%
Computers/ PCs with CD-ROMs	72.3%	85.7%	92.6%	75.9%	93.3%	100.0%	64.7%	80.0%	76.7%
Computers/ PCs with modems	60.0%	92.9%	88.9%	72.4%	100.0%	80.0%	58.8%	100.0%	80.0%
Laptops/ Notebooks/ Mobiles	30.8%	50.0%	88.9%	50.0%	100.0%	100.0%	47.1%	80.0%	76.7%
Total	227.7%	317.9%	366.7%	274.1%	380.0%	360.0%	235.3%	360.0%	323.3%

Table B19 Reasons for Not Using a PC (1=Most important) (Q2.3)

	Median	Mode
No need	1	1
IT too expensive	3	3
Need to know more about IT	2	1
Other	3	2

Table B20 Networking (Q2.4)

	Count	%
Yes	168	65.6%
No	88	34.4%
Total	256	100.0%

Table B21 Networking by Organisation Type (Q2.4)

	General Practice surveying	Quantity surveying	Corporate
Yes	62.0%	54.2%	92.3%
No	38.0%	45.8%	7.7%
Total	100.0%	100.0%	100.0%

Table B22 Networking by Organisation Type and Size (Q2.4)

	General Practice surveying			Quantity surveying			Corporate		
	Small (1-5)	Medium/ Large (6-20)	Very Large (>20)	Small (1-5)	Medium/ Large (6-20)	Very Large (>20)	Small (1-5)	Medium/ Large (6-20)	Very Large (>20)
Yes	37.9%	82.1%	100.0%	43.5%	86.7%	83.3%	76.5%	100.0%	100.0%
No	62.1%	17.9%		56.5%	13.3%	16.7%	23.5%		
Total	100.0%	100.0%	100.0%	100.0%	100.0%	100.0%	100.0%	100.0%	100.0%

Table B23 Reasons for Not Networking (Q2.5)

	Cases	Cases %
Only one computer/PC	36	42.4%
Currently networking	12	14.1%
No need for networking	33	38.8%
Networking is too expensive	5	5.9%
Networks are unreliable	1	1.2%
Need to improve understanding	8	9.4%
Total	85	111.8%

Table B24 Reasons for Not Networking by Organisation Type (Q2.5)

	General Practice surveying	Quantity surveying	Corporate
	Cases %	Cases %	Cases %
Only one computer/PC	42.6%	44.1%	25.0%
Currently networking	17.0%	8.8%	25.0%
No need for networking	38.3%	41.2%	25.0%
Networking is too expensive	2.1%	8.8%	25.0%
Networks are unreliable	2.1%		
Need to improve understanding	6.4%	14.7%	
Total	108.5%	117.6%	100.0%

| | General Practice surveying | | Quantity surveying | | Corporate |
| | Small (1-5) | Medium/ Large (6-20) | Small (1-5) | Medium/ Large (6-20) | Small (1-5) |
	Cases %	Cases %	Cases %	Cases %	Cases %
Only one computer/PC	47.6%		48.4%		25.0%
Currently networking	19.0%		3.2%	66.7%	25.0%
No need for networking	35.7%	60.0%	41.9%	33.3%	25.0%
Networking is too expensive		20.0%	9.7%		25.0%
Networks are unreliable	2.4%				
Need to improve understanding	2.4%	40.0%	16.1%		
Total	107.1%	120.0%	119.4%	100.0%	100.0%

Internet and Intranets

Table B26 Use of Email (Q3.1)

	Count	%
Not used-no PC	9	3.4%
Not used and no plans	22	8.4%
Not used but plans within 6 mths	30	11.5%
Not used but long term plans	20	7.7%
Rarely	12	4.6%
Occasionally	42	16.1%
Quite often	34	13.0%
Frequently	92	35.2%
Total	261	100.0%

Table B27 Use of Email by Organisation Type (Q3.1)

| | General Practice surveying | Quantity surveying | Corporate |
	%	%	%
Not used-no PC	2.4%	6.0%	1.9%
Not used and no plans	7.2%	10.7%	7.7%
Not used but plans within 6 mths	15.2%	9.5%	5.8%
Not used but long term plans	10.4%	3.6%	7.7%
Rarely	4.8%	3.6%	5.8%
Occasionally	16.8%	19.0%	9.6%
Quite often	12.8%	16.7%	7.7%
Frequently	30.4%	31.0%	53.8%
Total	100.0%	100.0%	100.0%

Table B28 Use of Email by Organisation Type and Size (Q3.1)

	General Practice surveying			Quantity surveying			Corporate		
	Small (1-5)	Medium /Large (6-20)	Very Large (>20)	Small (1-5)	Medium/ Large (6-20)	Very Large (>20)	Small (1-5)	Medium/ Large (6-20)	Very Large (>20)
Not used-no PC	4.3%			7.9%					3.3%
Not used and no plans	12.9%			14.3%			11.8%	20.0%	3.3%
Not used but plans within 6 mths	17.1%	25.0%		12.7%			5.9%	20.0%	3.3%
Not used but long term plans	17.1%	3.6%		4.8%			17.6%		3.3%
Rarely	5.7%	3.6%	3.7%	4.8%			11.8%		3.3%
Occasionally	15.7%	21.4%	14.8%	22.2%	13.3%		17.6%		6.7%
Quite often	11.4%	17.9%	11.1%	15.9%	26.7%				13.3%
Frequently	15.7%	28.6%	70.4%	17.5%	60.0%	100.0%	35.3%	60.0%	63.3%
Total	100.0%	100.0%	100.0%	100.0%	100.0%	100.0%	100.0%	100.0%	100.0%

Table B29 Reasons for Email Use (Q3.2)

	Cases	Cases %
Communication within a site	50	26.9%
Communication between local sites	55	29.6%
Communication between national sites	76	40.9%
Communication between international sites	40	21.5%
Communication with customers/clients	152	81.7%
Communication with others	97	52.2%
Other	3	1.6%
Total	186	254.3%

Table B30 Reasons for Email Use by Organisation Type (Q3.2)

	General Practice surveying	Quantity surveying	Corporate
	Cases %	Cases %	Cases %
Communication within a site	26.8%	17.5%	41.5%
Communication between local sites	37.8%	15.9%	34.1%
Communication between national sites	37.8%	39.7%	48.8%
Communication between international sites	25.6%	12.7%	26.8%
Communication with customers/clients	81.7%	90.5%	68.3%
Communication with others	43.9%	58.7%	58.5%
Other	3.7%		
Total	257.3%	234.9%	278.0%

Table B31 Reasons for Email Use by Organisation Type and Size (Q3.2)

	General Practice surveying			Quantity surveying			Corporate		
	Small (1-5)	Medium/ Large (6-20)	Very Large (>20)	Small (1-5)	Medium/ Large (6-20)	Very Large (>20)	Small (1-5)	Medium/ Large (6-20)	Very Large (>20)
	Cases %	Cases %	Cases %	Cases %	Cases %	Cases %	Cases %	Cases %	Cases %
Communication within a site	11.4%	33.3%	42.3%	7.1%	26.7%	66.7%	41.7%	66.7%	38.5%
Communication between local sites	42.9%	19.0%	46.2%	14.3%	6.7%	50.0%	41.7%	66.7%	26.9%
Communication between national sites	22.9%	42.9%	53.8%	33.3%	40.0%	83.3%	58.3%	100.0%	38.5%
Communication between international sites	17.1%	14.3%	46.2%	11.9%	6.7%	33.3%	25.0%	33.3%	26.9%
Communication with customers/clients	80.0%	76.2%	88.5%	92.9%	93.3%	66.7%	91.7%	33.3%	61.5%
Communication with others	37.1%	42.9%	53.8%	54.8%	66.7%	66.7%	41.7%	33.3%	69.2%
Other	2.9%	4.8%	3.8%						
Total	214.3%	233.3%	334.6%	214.3%	240.0%	366.7%	300.0%	333.3%	261.5%

Table B32 Reasons for Introducing Email (Q3.3) (1=Most Important)

	Median	Mode
To increase efficiency	1	1
Customers'/ clients' requests	2	3
To maintain competitive edge	2	2
Other	2	2

Table B33 Reasons for Introducing Email by Organisation Type (Q3.3) (1=Most Important)

	General Practice surveying	Quantity surveying	Corporate
	Median	Median	Median
To increase efficiency	1	1	1
Customers'/ clients' requests	2	2	3
To maintain competitive edge	2	2	2
Other	3	2	1

Table B34 Reasons for Introducing Email by Organisation Type and Size (Q3.3) (1=Most Important)

	General Practice surveying			Quantity surveying			Corporate		
	Small (1-5)	Medium/ Large (6-20)	Very Large (>20)	Small (1-5)	Medium/ Large (6-20)	Very Large (>20)	Small (1-5)	Medium/ Large (6-20)	Very Large (>20)
	Median	Median	Median	Median	Median	Median	Median	Median	Median
To increase efficiency	1	2	1	2	1	1	1	1	1
Customers'/ clients' requests	3	2	2	2	2	3	2	4	3
To maintain competitive edge	2	2	2	2	3	2	1	3	2
Other	2	3	4	2	2	.	.	2	1

Table B35 Access to the World Wide Web (Q3.4)

	Count	%
No access-intentions unknown	35	13.4%
No access and no plans	44	16.9%
No current access but within 6 mths	27	10.3%
Yes-access from shared PCs	117	44.8%
Yes- other access (single PC)	30	11.5%
No PC	8	3.1%
Total	261	100.0%

Table B36 Access to the World Wide Web by Organisation Type (Q3.4)

	General Practice surveying	Quantity surveying	Corporate
No access-intentions unknown	18.4%	9.5%	7.7%
No access and no plans	16.8%	17.9%	15.4%
No current access but within 6 mths	9.6%	14.3%	5.8%
Yes-access from shared PCs	44.0%	39.3%	55.8%
Yes- other access (single PC)	8.8%	13.1%	15.4%
No PC	2.4%	6.0%	
Total	100.0%	100.0%	100.0%

Table B37 Access to World Wide Web By Organisation Type and Size (Q3.4)

	General Practice surveying			Quantity surveying			Corporate		
	Small (1-5)	Medium/ Large (6-20)	Very Large (>20)	Small (1-5)	Medium/ Large (6-20)	Very Large (>20)	Small (1-5)	Medium/ Large (6-20)	Very Large (>20)
No access-intentions unknown	30.0%	3.6%	3.7%	12.7%				20.0%	10.0%
No access and no plans	18.6%	21.4%	7.4%	20.6%	6.7%	16.7%	23.5%	20.0%	10.0%
No current access but within 6 mths	10.0%	10.7%	7.4%	14.3%	20.0%		11.8%	20.0%	
Yes-access from shared PCs	31.4%	57.1%	63.0%	33.3%	60.0%	50.0%	58.8%	40.0%	56.7%
Yes- other access (single PC)	5.7%	7.1%	18.5%	11.1%	13.3%	33.3%	5.9%		23.3%
No PC	4.3%			7.9%					
Total	100.0%	100.0%	100.0%	100.0%	100.0%	100.0%	100.0%	100.0%	100.0%

Table B38 Use of World Wide Web (Q3.5)

	Cases	Cases %
Advertising/Marketing	68	40.7%
Marketing/ Comparables	42	25.1%
Research	124	74.3%
Business Contacts	55	32.9%
Information on Competitors	54	32.3%
News	86	51.5%
Market Trends	64	38.3%
Other	15	9.0%
Total	167	304.2%

Table B39 Use of World Wide Web by Organisation Type (Q3.5)

	General Practice surveying	Quantity surveying	Corporate
	Cases %	Cases %	Cases %
Advertising/ Marketing	48.7%	36.2%	31.0%
Marketing/ Comparables	33.3%	2.1%	35.7%
Research	71.8%	83.0%	69.0%
Business Contacts	23.1%	42.6%	40.5%
Information on Competitors	30.8%	25.5%	42.9%
News	56.4%	34.0%	61.9%
Market Trends	41.0%	27.7%	45.2%
Other	7.7%	8.5%	11.9%
Total	312.8%	259.6%	338.1%

Table B40 Use of World Wide Web by Organisation Type and Size (Q3.5)

	General Practice surveying			Quantity surveying			Corporate		
	Small (1-5)	Medium/ Large (6-20)	Very Large (>20)	Small (1-5)	Medium/ Large (6-20)	Very Large (>20)	Small (1-5)	Medium/ Large (6-20)	Very Large (>20)
	Cases %	Cases %	Cases %	Cases %	Cases %	Cases %	Cases %	Cases %	Cases %
Advertising/ Marketing	43.3%	52.4%	51.9%	31.0%	30.8%	80.0%	38.5%	33.3%	26.9%
Marketing/ Comparables	33.3%	33.3%	33.3%	3.4%			30.8%	33.3%	38.5%
Research	70.0%	61.9%	81.5%	75.9%	92.3%	100.0%	61.5%	33.3%	76.9%
Business Contacts	16.7%	23.8%	29.6%	44.8%	23.1%	80.0%	30.8%	33.3%	46.2%
Information on Competitors	16.7%	38.1%	40.7%	31.0%		60.0%	38.5%	66.7%	42.3%
News	40.0%	57.1%	74.1%	27.6%	38.5%	60.0%	46.2%	66.7%	69.2%
Market Trends	16.7%	52.4%	59.3%	27.6%	23.1%	40.0%	30.8%	66.7%	50.0%
Other	3.3%	19.0%	3.7%	10.3%		20.0%	7.7%	33.3%	11.5%
	240.0%	338.1%	374.1%	251.7%	207.7%	440.0%	284.6%	366.7%	361.5%

Table B41 Presence of Formal Internet Access Policy (Q3.6)

	Count	%
Yes	74	35.1%
No	137	64.9%
Total	211	100.0%

Base: Respondents with at least email access

Table B42 Presence of Formal Internet Access Policy by Organisation Type (Q3.6)

	General Practice surveying	Quantity surveying	Corporate
Yes	30.8%	30.4%	49.0%
No	69.2%	69.6%	51.0%
Total	100.0%	100.0%	100.0%

Base: Respondents with at least email access

Table B43 Presence of Formal Internet Access Policy by Organisation Type and Size (Q3.6)

	General Practice surveying			Quantity surveying			Corporate		
	Small (1-5)	Medium/ Large (6-20)	Very Large (>20)	Small (1-5)	Medium/ Large (6-20)	Very Large (>20)	Small (1-5)	Medium/ Large (6-20)	Very Large (>20)
Yes	15.8%	34.6%	48.1%	20.8%	33.3%	100.0%	41.2%	20.0%	58.6%
No	84.2%	65.4%	51.9%	79.2%	66.7%		58.8%	80.0%	41.4%
Total	100.0%	100.0%	100.0%	100.0%	100.0%	100.0%	100.0%	100.0%	100.0%

Base: Respondents with at least email access

Table B44 *Driving Force for World Wide Web Development (Q3.7)*

	Count	%
IT	66	40.7%
Marketing	38	23.5%
Other	58	35.8%
Total	162	100.0%

Base: Respondents with at least email access

Table B45 *Driving Force for World Wide Web Development by Organisation Type (Q3.7)*

	General Practice surveying	Quantity surveying	Corporate
IT	30.6%	48.1%	50.0%
Marketing	26.4%	20.4%	22.2%
Other	43.1%	31.5%	27.8%
Total	100.0%	100.0%	100.0%

Base: Respondents with at least email access

Table B46 *Driving Force for World Wide Web Development by Organisation Type and Size (Q3.7)*

	General Practice surveying			Quantity surveying			Corporate		
	Small (1-5)	Medium/ Large (6-20)	Very Large (>20)	Small (1-5)	Medium/ Large (6-20)	Very Large (>20)	Small (1-5)	Medium/ Large (6-20)	Very Large (>20)
IT	3.8%	23.8%	64.0%	40.0%	61.5%	66.7%	20.0%	66.7%	60.9%
Marketing	34.6%	23.8%	20.0%	25.7%	15.4%		30.0%		21.7%
Other	61.5%	52.4%	16.0%	34.3%	23.1%	33.3%	50.0%	33.3%	17.4%
Total	100.0%	100.0%	100.0%	100.0%	100.0%	100.0%	100.0%	100.0%	100.0%

Base: Respondents with at least email access

Table B47 *Site on the World Wide Web (Q3.8)*

	Count	%
Yes	86	34.0%
No	167	66.0%
Total	253	100.0%

Base: Respondents with PCs

Table B48 *Site on the World Wide Web by Organisation Type (Q3.8)*

	General Practice surveying	Quantity surveying	Corporate
Yes	33.6%	26.6%	46.2%
No	66.4%	73.4%	53.8%
Total	100.0%	100.0%	100.0%

Base: Respondents with PCs

Table B49 Site on the World Wide Web by Organisation Type and Size (Q3.8)

	General Practice surveying			Quantity surveying			Corporate		
	Small (1-5)	Medium/ Large (6-20)	Very Large (>20)	Small (1-5)	Medium/ Large (6-20)	Very Large (>20)	Small (1-5)	Medium/ Large (6-20)	Very Large (>20)
Yes	20.9%	42.9%	55.6%	20.7%	40.0%	50.0%	23.5%	60.0%	56.7%
No	79.1%	57.1%	44.4%	79.3%	60.0%	50.0%	76.5%	40.0%	43.3%
Total	100.0%	100.0%	100.0%	100.0%	100.0%	100.0%	100.0%	100.0%	100.0%

Base: Respondents with PCs

Table B50 Number of Hits per Month on WWW Site (Q3.8)

	Mean	Minimum	Maximum	Range
General Practice surveying	4849	10	80000	79990
Quantity surveying	324	10	2000	1990
Corporate	7956	50	30000	29950

Base: Respondents with Access to WWW

Table B51 Internet Service Providers (Q3.9)

	Count	%
Pipex	14	9.2%
Focus	9	5.9%
Planet	2	1.3%
BT	13	8.5%
Demon	29	19.0%
AOL	12	7.8%
UUNet	4	2.6%
Compuserve	18	11.8%
Other	52	34.0%
Total	153	100.0%

Base: Respondents with at least email access

Table B52 Internet Service Provider by Organisation Type(Q3.9)

	General Practice surveying	Quantity surveying	Corporate
Pipex	2.7%	9.6%	26.9%
Focus	10.7%		3.8%
Planet	2.7%		
BT	9.3%	5.8%	11.5%
Demon	20.0%	19.2%	15.4%
AOL	9.3%	5.8%	7.7%
UUNet	2.7%	3.8%	
Compuserve	6.7%	19.2%	11.5%
Other	36.0%	36.5%	23.1%
Total	100.0%	100.0%	100.0%

Base: Respondents with at least email access

Table B53 Year of Home Page Development (Q3.12)

	Count	%
1995	4	5.1%
1996	22	28.2%
1997	38	48.7%
1998	14	17.9%
Total	78	100.0%

Base: Respondents with WWW Access

Table B54 Year of Home Page Development by Organisation Type (Q3.12) (Number of organisations)

	General Practice surveying	Quantity surveying	Corporate
1995	1	2	1
1996	7	7	8
1997	23	9	6
1998	7	5	2
Total	38	23	17

Base: Respondents with WWW Access

Table B55 Presence of Intranet (Q3.15)

	Count	%
Yes	44	16.9%
No and no plans to do so	134	51.3%
No but plan within 6 mths	43	16.5%
No-no PC	8	3.1%
No-intentions unknown	32	12.3%
Total	261	100.0%

Table B56 Presence of Intranet by Organisation Type (Q3.15)

	General Practice surveying	Quantity surveying	Corporate
Yes	12.8%	6.0%	44.2%
No and no plans to do so	54.4%	57.1%	34.6%
No but plan within 6 mths	18.4%	15.5%	13.5%
No-no PC	2.4%	6.0%	
No-intentions unknown	12.0%	15.5%	7.7%
Total	100.0%	100.0%	100.0%

Table B57 Presence of Intranet by Organisation Type and Size (Q3.15)

	General Practice surveying			Quantity surveying			Corporate		
	Small (1-5)	Medium/ Large (6-20)	Very Large (>20)	Small (1-5)	Medium/ Large (6-20)	Very Large (>20)	Small (1-5)	Medium/ Large (6-20)	Very Large (>20)
Yes	1.4%	17.9%	37.0%	3.2%	6.7%	33.3%	29.4%	60.0%	50.0%
No and no plans to do so	61.4%	67.9%	22.2%	57.1%	66.7%	33.3%	52.9%	20.0%	26.7%
No but plan within 6 mths	12.9%	10.7%	40.7%	11.1%	26.7%	33.3%	11.8%		16.7%
No-no PC	4.3%			7.9%					
No-intentions unknown	20.0%	3.6%		20.6%			5.9%	20.0%	6.7%
Total	100.0%	100.0%	100.0%	100.0%	100.0%	100.0%	100.0%	100.0%	100.0%

Table B58 Use of Intranet (Q3.16)

	Responses	Cases %
Document transfer	26	55.3%
Company information	38	80.9%
Email	31	66.0%
Access to Websites	20	42.6%
Other	1	2.1%
Total	116	246.8%

Base: Respondents with Intranets

Table B59 Use of Intranet by Organisation Type (Q3.16)

	General Practice surveying	Quantity surveying	Corporate
	Cases %	Cases %	Cases %
Document transfer	47.1%	50.0%	62.5%
Company information	82.4%	50.0%	87.5%
Email	58.8%	66.7%	70.8%
Access to Websites	47.1%	50.0%	37.5%
Other	5.9%		
Total	241.2%	216.7%	258.3%

Base: Respondents with Intranets

Table B60 Use of Intranet by Organisation Type and Size (Q3.16)

	General Practice surveying			Quantity surveying			Corporate		
	Small (1-5)	Medium/ Large (6-20)	Very Large (>20)	Small (1-5)	Medium/ Large (6-20)	Very Large (>20)	Small (1-5)	Medium/ Large (6-20)	Very Large (>20)
	Cases %	Cases %	Cases %	Cases %	Cases %	Cases %	Cases %	Cases %	Cases %
Document transfer		20.0%	63.6%	66.7%	100.0%		60.0%	66.7%	62.5%
Company information	100.0%	60.0%	90.9%	33.3%		100.0%	100.0%	66.7%	87.5%
Email		80.0%	54.5%	100.0%	100.0%		60.0%	100.0%	68.8%
Access to Websites		20.0%	63.6%	66.7%		50.0%	40.0%		43.8%
Other			9.1%						
Total	100.0%	180.0%	281.8%	266.7%	200.0%	150.0%	260.0%	233.3%	262.5%

Base: Respondents with Intranets

Table B61 Intranet Linkage (Q3.17)

	Count	%
No	7	16.3%
Yes-in the UK	26	60.5%
Yes-internationally	10	23.3%
Total	43	100.0%

Base: Respondents with Intranets

Table B62 Intranet Linkage by Organisation Type (Q3.17)

	General Practice surveying	Quantity surveying	Corporate
No		50.0%	17.4%
Yes-in the UK	85.7%	50.0%	47.8%
Yes-internationally	14.3%		34.8%
Total	100.0%	100.0%	100.0%

Base: Respondents with Intranets

Table B63 Intranet Linkage by Organisation Type and Size (Q3.17)

	General Practice surveying			Quantity surveying			Corporate		
	Small (1-5)	Medium/ Large (6-20)	Very Large (>20)	Small (1-5)	Medium/ Large (6-20)	Very Large (>20)	Small (1-5)	Medium/ Large (6-20)	Very Large (>20)
No				50.0%		66.7%	60.0%		6.7%
Yes-in the UK		100.0%	77.8%	50.0%	100.0%	33.3%		100.0%	53.3%
Yes-internationally			22.2%				40.0%		40.0%
Total		100.0%	100.0%	100.0%	100.0%	100.0%	100.0%	100.0%	100.0%

Base: Respondents with Intranets

Table B64 Year of Intranet Development (Q3.18)

	Count	%
1995	6	20%
1996	5	16.7%
1997	11	36.7%
1998	8	26.7%
Total	30	100.0%

Base: Respondents with Intranets

Table B65 Year of Intranet Development by Organisation Type (Q3.18)

	General Practice surveying	Quantity surveying	Corporate
1995	1		5
1996	2		3
1997	4		7
1998	4	1	3
Total	11	1	18

Base: Respondents with Intranets

Table B66 Driving Force for Intranet (Q3.19)

	Count	%
IT	28	68.3%
Marketing	2	4.9%
Other	11	26.8%
Total	41	100.0%

Base: Respondents with Intranets

Table B67 Driving Force for Intranet by Organisation Type (Q3.19)

	General Practice surveying	Quantity surveying	Corporate
	%	%	%
IT	64.3%	75.0%	69.6%
Marketing	7.1%		4.3%
Other	28.6%	25.0%	26.1%
Total	100.0%	100.0%	100.0%

Base: Respondents with Intranets

Table B68 Barriers to the Internet (4=Very Important) (Q3.13)

	Mean	Median	Mode
Lack of security	(2.93)	3	4
Speed	(2.93)	3	3
Threat to professional work	(2.04)	2	1
Congestion	(2.39)	2	2
Costs	(2.51)	2	2
Too much information	(2.35)	2	2
Legal/confidentiality issues	(2.68)	3	4
Other	(3.23)	4	4

Base: Respondents with PCs

Table B69 Barriers to the Internet by Organisation Type (4=Very Important) (Q3.13)

	General Practice surveying	Quantity surveying	Corporate
	Mean	Mean	Mean
Lack of security	(2.83)	(2.83)	(3.30)
Speed	(2.88)	(3.05)	(2.83)
Threat to professional work	(2.00)	(2.11)	(2.00)
Congestion	(2.38)	(2.49)	(2.28)
Costs	(2.48)	(2.54)	(2.53)
Too much information	(2.44)	(2.25)	(2.29)
Legal/confidentiality issues	(2.62)	(2.53)	(3.02)
Other	(3.00)	(3.67)	(4.00)

Base: Respondents with PCs

Table B70 Barriers to the Internet by Organisation Type and Size (4=Very Important) (Q3.13)

	General Practice surveying			Quantity surveying			Corporate		
	Small (1-5)	Medium / Large (6-20)	Very Large (>20)	Small (1-5)	Medium/ Large (6-20)	Very Large (>20)	Small (1-5)	Medium/ Large (6-20)	Very Large (>20)
	Mean	Mean	Mean	Mean	Mean	Mean	Mean	Mean	Mean
Lack of security	(2.53)	(3.09)	(3.08)	(2.82)	(2.73)	(3.17)	(2.83)	(3.25)	(3.52)
Speed	(2.97)	(2.76)	(2.84)	(3.05)	(3.07)	(3.00)	(2.83)	(2.75)	(2.85)
Threat to professional work	(1.93)	(1.95)	(2.17)	(2.21)	(1.87)	(2.00)	(2.00)	(2.50)	(1.92)
Congestion	(2.30)	(2.38)	(2.50)	(2.53)	(2.47)	(2.33)	(2.25)	(2.50)	(2.25)
Costs	(2.42)	(2.71)	(2.35)	(2.67)	(2.33)	(2.00)	(2.82)	(2.75)	(2.36)
Too much information	(2.63)	(2.29)	(2.26)	(2.24)	(2.27)	(2.33)	(2.42)	(2.25)	(2.24)
Legal/ confidentiality issues	(2.51)	(2.85)	(2.61)	(2.56)	(2.53)	(2.33)	(2.83)	(2.50)	(3.20)
Other	(2.80)	(4.00)	(3.25)	(3.67)	(4.00)	(3.00)	(.)	(.)	(4.00)

Base: Respondents with PCs

Table B71 Barriers to the Internet By Web Access (4=Very Important) (Q3.13)

	No Access	With Access
	Mean	Mean
Lack of security	2.93	2.94
Speed	2.78	2.98
Threat to professional work	2.34	1.92
Congestion	2.31	2.42
Costs	2.79	2.36
Too much information	2.31	2.35
Legal/confidentiality issues	3.02	2.52
Other	2.83	2.83

Base: Respondents with PCs

Table B72 Benefits of the Internet (4=Very Important) (Q3.14)

	Median	Mode	Mean
Increased revenue	2	1	(2.28)
Increased productivity	3	3	(2.78)
Reduced communication costs	3	4	(2.86)
Reduced cost of sharing information	3	3	(2.83)
Increased competitive advantage	3	3	(3.10)
Other	4	4	(3.17)

Base: Respondents with at least Email access

Table B73 Benefits of the Internet by Organisation Type (4=Very Important) (Q3.14)

	Corporate	Quantity surveying	General Practice surveying
	Mean	Mean	Mean
Increased revenue	(2.16)	(2.08)	(2.47)
Increased productivity	(2.79)	(2.85)	(2.74)
Reduced communication costs	(2.68)	(2.91)	(2.92)
Reduced cost of sharing information	(2.85)	(2.69)	(2.92)
Increased competitive advantage	(2.84)	(3.09)	(3.24)
Other	(3.00)	(3.60)	(2.80)

Base: Respondents with at least Email access

Table B74 Benefits of the Internet by Organisation Type and Size (4=Very Important) (Q3.14)

	General Practice surveying			Quantity surveying			Corporate		
	Small (1-5)	Medium/ Large (6-20)	Very Large (>20)	Small (1-5)	Medium/ Large (6-20)	Very Large (>20)	Small (1-5)	Medium/ Large (6-20)	Very Large (>20)
	Mean	Mean	Mean	Mean	Mean	Mean	Mean	Mean	Mean
Increased revenue	(2.22)	(2.74)	(2.64)	(2.10)	(1.93)	(2.40)	(2.36)	(2.25)	(2.04)
Increased productivity	(2.66)	(2.74)	(2.87)	(2.76)	(3.00)	(3.00)	(2.91)	(3.00)	(2.70)
Reduced communication costs	(2.87)	(2.84)	(3.10)	(2.84)	(3.27)	(2.40)	(2.92)	(2.50)	(2.60)
Reduced cost of sharing information	(2.73)	(3.16)	(3.05)	(2.59)	(3.07)	(2.20)	(2.45)	(2.75)	(3.04)
Increased competitive advantage	(3.11)	(3.53)	(3.22)	(3.09)	(3.07)	(3.20)	(2.90)	(3.00)	(2.79)
Other	(2.00)	(4.00)	(4.00)	(3.50)	(4.00)	(.)	(3.00)	(.)	(.)

Base: Respondents with at least Email access

Additional Questions

Table B75 Factors Promoting Internet and Intranet (4=Very Important) (Q4.1)

	Mean	Median	Mode
Existing IT culture	(2.71)	3	3
Senior management support	(3.03)	3	3
Involvement of all staff	(2.42)	2	2
Formal IT strategy	(2.39)	3	3
Linkage to business plan	(2.21)	2	3
Training/education plan	(2.28)	2	3
Other	(3.00)	3	4

Base: Respondents with Email and/or Web Access

Table B76 Factors Promoting Internet and Intranet by Organisation Type (4=Very Important) (Q4.1)

	General Practice surveying	Quantity surveying	Corporate
	Mean	Mean	Mean
Existing IT culture	(2.62)	(2.71)	(2.90)
Senior management support	(3.02)	(2.85)	(3.29)
Involvement of all staff	(2.47)	(2.33)	(2.45)
Formal IT strategy	(2.23)	(2.34)	(2.73)
Linkage to business plan	(2.18)	(2.09)	(2.46)
Training/education plan	(2.34)	(2.10)	(2.39)
Other	(2.71)	(3.33)	(3.33)

Base: Respondents with Email and/or Web Access

Table B77 Factors Promoting Internet and Intranet by Organisation Type and Size (4=Very Important) (Q4.1)

	General Practice surveying			Quantity surveying			Corporate		
	Small (1-5)	Medium/ Large (6-20)	Very Large (>20)	Small (1-5)	Medium /Large (6-20)	Very Large (>20)	Small (1-5)	Medium/ Large (6-20)	Very Large (>20)
	Mean	Mean	Mean	Mean	Mean	Mean	Mean	Mean	Mean
Existing IT culture	(2.46)	(2.45)	(3.00)	(2.54)	(3.08)	(3.00)	(2.83)	(3.00)	(2.92)
Senior management support	(2.92)	(3.05)	(3.16)	(2.75)	(3.00)	(3.17)	(3.07)	(3.33)	(3.42)
Involvement of all staff	(2.31)	(2.55)	(2.63)	(2.31)	(2.38)	(2.33)	(2.42)	(2.67)	(2.43)
Formal IT strategy	(1.63)	(2.10)	(3.08)	(2.06)	(2.85)	(2.83)	(2.62)	(3.33)	(2.72)
Linkage to business plan	(1.81)	(2.33)	(2.57)	(2.03)	(2.31)	(2.00)	(2.55)	(3.33)	(2.30)
Training/education plan	(1.97)	(2.58)	(2.67)	(2.06)	(2.17)	(2.17)	(2.67)	(2.67)	(2.22)
Other	(1.75)	(4.00)	(4.00)	(2.00)	(4.00)	(.)	(3.00)	(.)	(3.50)

Base: Respondents with Email and/or Web Access

Table B78 Views/The Future (4=Agree Strongly) (Q4.2)

	Mean	Median	Mode
Internet will replace surveyors role	(1.73)	2	2
Internet will soon impact on clients	(2.19)	2	2
Surveyors must understand the Internet	(3.09)	3	4

Table B79 Views/The Future by Organisation Type (4=Agree Strongly) (Q4.2)

	General Practice surveying	Quantity surveying	Corporate
	Mean	Mean	Mean
Internet will replace surveyors role	(1.70)	(1.59)	(2.02)
Internet will soon impact on clients	(2.21)	(2.23)	(2.09)
Surveyors must understand the Internet	(3.14)	(2.92)	(3.23)

Table B80 B79 Views/The Future by Organisation Type and Size (4=Agree Strongly) (Q4.2)

	General Practice surveying			Quantity surveying			Corporate		
	Small (1-5)	Medium/ Large (6-20)	Very Large (>20)	Small (1-5)	Medium/ Large (6-20)	Very Large (>20)	Small (1-5)	Medium/ Large (6-20)	Very Large (>20)
	Mean	Mean	Mean	Mean	Mean	Mean	Mean	Mean	Mean
Internet will replace surveyors role	(1.71)	(1.64)	(1.73)	(1.55)	(1.50)	(2.17)	(2.00)	(2.25)	(2.00)
Internet will soon impact on clients	(2.17)	(2.25)	(2.23)	(2.20)	(2.40)	(2.17)	(2.13)	(2.50)	(2.00)
Surveyors must understand the Internet	(3.00)	(3.21)	(3.42)	(2.82)	(3.27)	(3.00)	(3.20)	(3.75)	(3.18)

APPENDIX 3: ADDITIONAL COMMENTS FROM POSTAL QUESTIONNAIRE RESPONDENTS

Will be an essential tool of the trade.

Young surveyors expect access.

Major impact on surveyors when clients embrace it.
At present usage is unstructured-needs more formal.

Yet to fully comprehend the range of opportunities/challenge.

Ability to access/analyse information is crucial-Internet aids this

Lack of structure. Email useful not WWW
Will never take the place of interpretation of information

Good for low value dissemination of information. Does not threaten professional services.

Enables firm to transmit report/documents to clients. Reduces paper copy and speeds process of 'instruction-survey-report-client'.

Lack of knowledge and shortage of appropriate training will leave most surveyors disadvantaged.

Information is the key to make good business decisions and increasing market share. We plan to go onto the Internet in 1998 because we know we have to in order to remain competitive.

Senior surveyors wake up!

It's a tool. Like any other it can be abused. I'm not convinced of the advantages of Internet/Intranet to our core business.

I am not sure it will have any effect but it may be useful for surveyors in obtaining information.

Need to be more accessible.

Email now a vital communication tool even for a very small practice. Other Internet opportunities are relevant to larger concerns.

It's a great time-waster unless one is presumably a global company!

Only relevant (at present) to large/national/international companies not small firms.

It is minimal at the moment.

IT is merely one of many marketing/communication media. The RICS will need to more to coordinate the use of the Internet within the profession.

Probably good for general information and awareness but not for individual clients.

Eventually it will broaden the knowledge available to all surveyors and be available quickly.

The Internet may be of use to the profession dependent on it proving its worth as opposed to a novelty. I am personally not aware of one deal that has been done via the Internet.

I am yet to be convinced it will be used to the extent predicted by experts. As a small firm we see it purely as a form of national advertising.

For local management firms there is no substitute for face-to-face client/tenant contact. Availability of information will increase. It is very slow to use and does not always give the desired result i.e. I would like to see easy access to market trends and for it to be a bit more like Focus.

We are looking to the RICS to extend its information services. Security problems are very underrated.

Without training human error will cause problems.

As a young company we are looking for additional sources of information, but cannot waste time. More basic quality, not 'high brow' information is required. The more time you spend playing around with the Internet the less time you have to get on with your work.

At present its use and operation are time-consuming.

Internet will provide a more efficient information provider, but the surveyor's skills will be needed for interpretation.

Surveyors must utilise this technology or they will become dinosaurs.

The Internet is much hyped. Very little impact expected in the property industry.

Limited impact on residential surveying other than as communication tool. Our surveyors can access the Web from Information Services (on 7th floor), but they rarely bother.

Enables quick, effective communication both nationally and internationally.

We are only just looking at rolling it out.

The surveying profession, in many areas, is still far behind where it should be.

We will join when many more have joined!

It will be used for all the purposes for which surface mail is used, and use will increase as speed increases.The Internet cannot measure, analyse or deduce.

It is an additional form of communication more suitable for transmission of professional information than to replace traditional agency / communication. There is room in the market for more functionality, for example property based services, on the Internet.

No real impact in the short to medium term.

Improvements in information management will not replace judgement but will aid productivity

The Internet/Intranet will be as influential as the other elements of our IT. Without the support of other technology it will be an expensive hobby.

The worldwide access to the net will have little impact to my business which is within a limited area.

A very useful database of information on all related topics.

Excellent for speeding up message leaving and sending of documents. What is legal status of an email instruction to a contractor?

Another source of information.

Requirement for standard industry software to make information transfer easier.

When connection calls are free and searching is faster there will be a big impact.

Internet's use as a major marketing tool is questionable, but will be highly valuable for information transfer.

Younger surveyors are 'Internet aware'. Older surveyors are falling behind.

The use of Web technology will allow the sharing of 'knowledge' in a much more pertinent way than has been possible before.

Still not widely used - limitations on information exchange.

APPENDIX 4: CASE STUDY INTERVIEWS

Case Study 1

Medium Sized General Practice Firm (Interviewee: Head of Research)

Evolution of the Internet

The Internet was first introduced in this organisation in 1995. The research department was given responsibility for developing the Internet link with partnership support. Although there is an IT department this acted purely as support. The system was email driven and built on a pre-existing network which linked every office. Primarily email was seen as a way of improving inter-office communication as well as communication with clients.

Home Page

The company home page was developed externally in July 1997 and has been primarily designed to describe the services offered by the company. Essentially, the research department saw that other companies were producing Web sites and decided to develop their own to obtain a higher profile. The home page is also used for auction sales and general marketing.

The Internet is seen very much as a tool for effecting transactions but as yet the company is not aware of any commercial property deal being struck on the Internet.

Using the Internet and the Impact on Professional Work

Professional staff have access to EGi and Focusnet which are used for news, deals, research and general information retrieval. The Internet is seen as a tool to aid the surveyor's work. It is unlikely that disintermediation will result because of the key problem of secrecy and confidentiality of deals/transactions. If there was a free flow of information then the threat to surveyors would be more substantial.   Nonetheless, the development of available site databases (e.g. Brownfield Site Database to be set up by DETR) may have an impact on site finders in companies.

Email also offered key advantages, but the speed of transactions was still slow because of the legal processes involved.

The Internet has not changed organisational structure.

Critical Success Factors

In developing the Internet it is vital to have an overall goal or aim. Keeping the Web site up-to-date is essential and it is crucial to have a 'champion for change' who takes overall responsibility for its introduction. Monitoring the effect of advertising is important . The benefits of a home page seem to be mainly 'soft' or intangible. The overall cost has been about £10000 to £20000.

In terms of developing a Web site it is important to be firm in carrying the design forward. Initially there were problems with staff wanting to change and edit the home page too frequently.

Currently there is a one PC to two staff ratio and this applies to all staff; in terms of Internet access the ratio is 1:10. Staff are able to access email and the World Wide Web. There is no Internet access policy and no formal training in IT for staff. A policy of trust operates for Internet use.

Future Development

Currently the Internet offers sites that are very often dated-particularly in property sales. It would be interesting to research into the impact of Internet property advertising. Smaller companies may find it difficult to get on the ladder because of costs but the benefits are real.

Case Study 2

Very Large International Surveying Practice (Interviewee: IT Manager)

Evolution of the Internet

The Internet was first implemented in the organisation in January 1997. The original justification was for email which developed form an internal email system implemented in 1991, and the World Wide Web followed soon after. The company also has an Intranet system. All professional staff have Internet access and Intranet access. The driving force for the Internet has been the IT board.

Home Page

The company home page was set up in mid 1997 and external consultancy has been used for the artistic design of the page. There is now a full-time member of staff who is responsible for Internet and Intranet development. Originally the site was developed for general marketing purposes, and there was an element of 'me too' in wanting to stay ahead of the competition.

There have been three 'generations' of development: IT and marketing led; transfer to marketing and then Marketing-led with IT support. It is considered vital keeping the information up-to-date.

Using the Internet and the Impact on Professional Work

Professional staff have access to EGi and Focusnet. Links are made using the Intranet. Internet use has not changed the organisational structure. The company, like other surveying practices tends to have a flat structure with teams working on projects. Communications with clients has improved dramatically however with the use of email.

It is very unlikely the Internet will cause disintermediation because of the complexity of transactions, the quality of advice needed in investment property. The Internet will help to market property indirectly and greater openness in deals/transactions would lead to greater use.

Critical Success Factors

Having a formal strategy can be a hindrance to Internet development although an overall aim is vital. Formalising a strategy can lead to no development. The following were important to bear in mind:

1. It is often difficult to come up with a good business case so if the soft benefits are important it is better just to go ahead and develop.
2. Do not be worried about trusting people over Internet access-the company has a liberal policy and does not restrict Internet use.
3. Downloading software should however be controlled as viruses and software problems could arise. This can be difficult with an access policy based on trust.
4. There is a need to make people aware of security over emailing clients with sensitive documents.
5. Technical impact is important but the technology can usually cope.
6. There is a need to involve the business in designing the Internet/Intranet.

The Internet system has cost about £40-50,000 in total to date.

Training and education are important and the company's information centre is very keen to promote this aspect by holding 'cyber-breakfasts'. A policy of trust operates for Internet use.

Future Development

The company has an Intranet which has been developed from existing technology. The Intranet includes external Internet access to outside links; internal access to databases and client information and an image library for presentations. The Intranet has been branded and is marketed internally to all staff. The next phase in its development is a discussion forum or bulletin board for divisional company work.

Case Study 3

Medium/Large General Practice Firm (Interviewee: Senior Partner)

Evolution of the Internet

Email was first introduced in the organisation in 1995 and built on the pre-existing network. The organisation also has access to the Web for all its professional staff. There are no requirements for a separate IT department and this function is outsourced to an external company.

Home Page

The home page was developed in 1995 using an external consultant and offers a summary of the services of the company. The partnership was the driving force for the introduction of email and the home page and the Internet had proved successful with US clients.

There was an element of staying ahead of the competition in setting up the home page. The home page has not really evolved since its original development, but there are plans to introduce an Intranet as a pilot project based around auctions in the near future. It is felt that this is ideal because of the relatively short lead-in time and the ability of the Internet to reach a wider audience. This development may require a full-time Webmaster.

Using the Internet and the Impact on Professional Work

Professional staff have access to EGi and Focusnet. These are supplemented by ICC and Hemscott which give financial and company information. The Internet is a valuable information retrieval tool for finding data, searching out contacts and legal advice. Using the Internet to market commercial property, however, implies the surveyor does not know his market: the approach could be too unfocused in its targeting. Disintermediation would not result in the commercial because of the skills still needed to interpret the data and information available. Data overload could become a problem, however.

The Internet has not changed organisational structure.

Critical Success Factors

It is important to have an overall aim in mind and a willingness to embrace the new technology. Enthusiasm from the partnership is important and training and education are also important. Having a permanent link made speed problems not an issue. A self-policing Internet access policy was in operation and there were other risks. A partner could, for example, set up a home page and do business outside the partnership. A company firewall and virus-checking of emails helped reduce other risks.

Education and training was implemented when a major upgrade occurred. 'Cascade' training also worked well in the organisation.

Future Development

In the mid to long term the Internet and other new technology may well affect markets in the City of London, but the impact on retailing would be less. The role of the surveyor would continue but would have to shift in emphasis as market information becomes more readily available.

Case Study 4

Very Large International Surveying Practice (Interviewee: IT Manager)

Evolution of the Internet

The Internet is based around email which was revamped 2 years ago. All staff are on email and there is restricted Web access for professional staff. The IT department is a key driving force for change but the Internet is just one small facet of the IT strategy for the company.

Home Page

A separate home page was developed by an overseas partner in 1996. The company was one of the first to go down this route. The page is not seen as dramatically adding to the client base, but is a way of advertising the services of the company to the wider world. Certainly there was an element of 'me, too' in setting up the page.

The use of email is critical in reducing paper flows to a minimum in the company.

Using the Internet and the Impact on Professional Work

Professional staff have access to EGi and Focus, and the Web is used as a means of providing information rather than marketing property. The company does, however, take space in EGi Propertylink for marketing property. The company is developing an Extranet to link with clients and interface with them to provide more relevant data/information. Email is a vital tool in the organisation but the culture of IT is very different in surveying, compared to the corporate world.

The Internet has not in itself changed organisational structure but has changed the way in which data/information is exchanged. Clients are much better-informed and the IT strategy is designed to enhance this process. The aim is to capture, present, and analyse information and present it to clients.

Critical Success Factors

Getting a site up to promote the company is a very cost-effective way of advertising. Although speed and congestion are criticisms the advantages outweigh the disadvantages. Getting online can also show how competitors are working and in itself offers lessons for the user. Marketing properties is likely to be less successful, particularly if it is commercial, because of the time-lags involved.

Future Development

Interpreting data/information will become more important. Whilst the company has a relatively flat structure already, the working environment will change for its employees. Floorspace savings resulting from the new technology was now a reality and the company was looking at this.

Case Study 5

Medium Sized General Practice Firm (Interviewee: Head of Research)

Evolution of the Internet

The introduction of the Internet was driven by the research and information department. Email and Web access was initially restricted until late 1996 when staff changes brought a change of personnel with corporate experience of IT. Since then email and Web access has increased so that professional staff have access if they wish.

Home Page

The company Home Page was developed in 1997 and was based around a CD-ROM marketing product developed externally. The Business Development Committee took responsibility for the development. The home page contains information on the services provided by the company but no property details. There is some debate in the organisation as to whether such details should be included, but the agency department feels that tracking clients would be more difficult than with a paper-based system. The site has remained unchanged since its inception and was introduced with partnership support to stay ahead of the pack.

Using the Internet and the Impact on Professional Work

Professional staff have access to EGi and Focus and access is gradually being opened up. There is a draft Internet access policy being developed. There is a mistrust and fear of new technology amongst some senior partners who do not use PCs. Some feel secrecy/confidentiality issues will be exacerbated by the Internet and others feel the surveyor's role will be diminished. However, others felt that in an open market clients can get hold of data and would still require analysis and expert knowledge.

The organisation had not changed structurally as a result of the Internet. Assistants were using the Internet to service partners who often felt they did not need to use it themselves.

Critical Success Factors

Having a 'champion for change' was clearly important in this organisation. Getting connected is easy and worthwhile to see how other Web sites had been set up. Senior partner support often has to be won over particularly from more senior members who remain unconvinced by IT. Although the research department was keen to promote staff training generally the company did not promote training actively.
Staff tended to teach themselves and there was no Internet training.

Future Development

The surveyor's role would inevitably change, particularly if barriers to data availability were lifted. It was likely that the number of information/data suppliers would also reduce through competition.

Case Study 6

Large Quantity Surveying Firm

Evolution of the Internet

The Internet has evolved over the last 2½ years to the present day situation where some 400 staff are connected with Exchange email facilities. Email has superseded many of the paper-based systems that were used. For example project based work involving collaborative teams uses email for drawings and other material. Staff do not have world wide Web access as the partnership and the IT department decided staff would waste time in surfing the net. Instead online services (e.g. Building online) are provided within the Exchange system. A separate information department provides further research support.

Home Page

The home page was designed within the Property Mall gateway as the first step towards providing Internet facilities. The main driving force for this was the partnership but the Web site is a marketing tool, and it is recognised that it requires revamping.

Using the Internet and the Impact on Professional Work

Those who were against the use of email because of confidentiality issues are not confirmed users. The technology is too new for it to change organisational structure to any extent. However, email has provided surveyors in the organisation with greater autonomy. It is likely that better technical systems will have an impact in the future and this will be important for measurement and communications.

The nature of the QS role makes it less likely that the Internet will impact on staff levels, although other structural changes within the organisation may be important in the future.

Critical Success Factors

Winning partnership support and persuading partners to accept change has been an important factor in ensuring success. There is a formal IT strategy in place and training and education is provided in house for staff. A major issue for this QS firm has been ensuring compatibility with the interchange of data over such differing systems as PIMS, BT construct and CADWEB.

The organisation is also exploring the possibility of Intranet use which would ensure, for example that a library of photographs was shared throughout the organisation. This will be constructed around the Exchange system.

Future Development

The It department is seen as fulfilling a core role in the organisation. Despite resistance to change the development of new systems within the organisation has had an enabling effect for professional staff and the company intends to reinforce these changes over the next few years

Case Study 7

Very Large International Surveying Practice

Evolution of the Internet

Email was the first element to be introduced some 3 years ago, and all staff have access to email with shared facilities to Focus and EGi. Email is used extensively throughout the organisation and has eliminated internal memoranda. It is increasingly used by clients and comes through the home page also.

Home Page

The home page was developed in 1996 and was driven by the IT partner and the Marketing department. A team of professional designers was employed to develop the home page. There has been some debate as to the function of the Web site, and it is currently being revamped. As the organisation is international it was felt that the home page was too UK orientated and so a .com extension will be implemented. It is difficult to judge the impact of the Internet on marketing properties but PropertyLink had proved to be a cost-effective way of reaching a global audience although the marketing was still in its infancy.

The company has a full-time Web master to update the home page.

Using the Internet and the Impact on Professional Work

The company has had a pervasive IT culture for some time and this has helped formulate an Internet strategy. Email and the Web have not changed the organisational structure but it is likely that a greater availability of information would shift the emphasis of the surveyors role. The company's organisational structure has not changed as a result of the Internet.

Critical Success Factors

having a formal IT strategy and senior partnership support appears to have worked well for this organisation. IT is at the heart of the business and a hierarchical approach to implementing IT by involving users had been used. 'IT champions' in each department were important in driving ideas forward. The organisation is young and graduates want to use the new technology.

This organisation had clearly found the Internet had benefited them, and from a PR point of view the home page had reached a wide audience. It was felt that further research on the impact of Internet advertising was required.

Training and Education was also important and this was often outsourced to external trainers. New employees must have training before using their PCs.

The company was in the process of implementing an Intranet which may be extended to form an Extranet (or series of Intranets). The intention is to give the organisation a competitive edge as part of continuous process of change.

Updating property details was important and a full-time Webmaster was employed for this function. It was vital to consider the Property Misdescriptions Act for such systems and also in an international context.

The organisation does not have a draconian Internet access policy (i.e. a parental guidance system) but has a firewall because confidentiality is an important issue. Monitoring is being carried out of Internet use by employees to minimise abuse.

Future Development

To take an example, residential buyers will not just look at the Internet and buy a property. The Internet gives people the opportunity to have access to better information but it is a means to an end.

Remote working and teleworking will not impact on the surveyors role but may have an impact on clients property requirements over the next 5-10 years.

Case Study 8

Large Property Company (Interviewee: IT and Research Officer)

Evolution of the Internet

The Internet has evolved only gradually within this organisation over the last 2-3 years. Currently only 1-2 PCs are used for Internet access and these are not networked. Some external email is sent but there are no plans for an Intranet, although the company has an IT department.

Home Page

The home page was developed in 1995 through Property Mall. It provides corporate information with some details on lettings and leasing opportunities. The site was partly influenced by US driven requests for information. The cost of the home page was £10,000-£15,000.

Using the Internet and the Impact on Professional Work.

There is very limited access to EGi and Focus within the organisation and so organisational structure has not been affected.

Critical Success Factors

In terms of home page development it is important to liaise fully with the designer to ensure success. Security risks were perceived as a key barrier to company-wide email. Also providing full Internet access could waste employees valuable time. There was a need to overcome 'techno-fear' amongst the company directors.

Future Development

The Internet could lead to changes in organisations. In particular the agent's role would inevitably diminish particularly if tenants were able to use the Web to access lettings details direct from Property companies.